PING!

PING!

DELICIOUS MICROWAVE
MEALS IN MINUTES

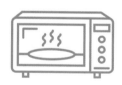

JUSTINE
PATTISON

CONTENTS

INTRODUCTION

Welcome to my cookbook! I'm so happy that you wanted to explore my microwave recipes and am looking forward to introducing you to what may be a whole new way of cooking!

This book is all about making the most of your microwave. A huge number of us – over 90% of households – own a microwave in the UK, but most people only use it to reheat leftovers and ready meals, or perhaps cook the odd jacket potato or frozen peas. I want to show you just how much can be achieved using your microwave – from stews with dumplings to delicious cakes, you will be amazed by the results.

Microwave cooking was very popular in the 1980s, when the first ovens started being sold in large numbers, and gave rise to the huge increase in chilled ready meals sold in every supermarket. But over the years, we have forgotten that microwave energy can also be used to cook fantastic dishes from scratch.

And the microwave method is for everyone – whether you are looking for the convenience of a quick home-cooked meal, are trying to save on energy costs by using your traditional oven and hob less, or are new to cooking and want some fool-proof ideas, this book is for you.

All the recipes have been carefully tried and tasted several times in my test kitchen, using different microwave ovens, so you can be sure they'll work just as well for you at home. To make the recipes even more accessible, I've only used ingredients that are easy to find and don't cost the earth. You'll also only require basic cooking equipment, and you don't need a fancy microwave either. All these dishes can be prepared in the most basic of models.

I hope that by following my recipes you'll discover how your microwave oven can work harder for you – and make life a whole lot simpler. You'll also have the added bonus of amazing your family and friends with what you can achieve in a microwave oven – that might sound a bit over the top, but I've seen it happen!

For more recipes, videos, tips and kitchen shortcuts, visit my website: **justinepattison.com.**

Happy microwaving!

Justine x

WHY MICROWAVE?

Before we start, here are my top seven reasons to start cooking from scratch in your microwave.

CONVENIENCE

Microwave cooking is incredibly convenient. Not only is food cooked in a much shorter time, you can also cook, serve, store and even freeze recipes in the same dish. And because food doesn't get baked on, as it would in a conventional oven or pan on the hob, washing up is so much easier, too.

SIMPLICITY

When I first started cooking, it was timing everything that I found most difficult. But with these recipes, I've worked out the timings for you. So, as long as you can press the right buttons, or turn the right knob, these dishes will be perfectly cooked. If you walk away or get distracted by something else, it doesn't matter, as the microwave will switch itself off. You can just carry on cooking when you return.

ENERGY SAVING

Using an oven for a long cooking time, making a casserole for instance, will cost so much more than making the same dish in the microwave. So, if you are keen to save money on energy bills, think about swapping a few meals a week to the microwave.

SPEED

Using a microwave will cut the cooking time of many of your favourite dishes drastically, so when you are busy, it makes sense to make the most of it.

CLEAN AIR

It might seem strange, but cooking in a microwave will also release fewer cooking smells into the kitchen than cooking in a conventional oven. This could be a real bonus if your house is open-plan and you are tired of lingering cooking smells.

COOLER KITCHEN

When it's sweltering hot, standing over the hob or even just having the oven on is the last thing you want to be doing. Cooking in a microwave will help to keep your kitchen – and you – a whole lot cooler. The shorter cooking time and the lack of direct heat means a lot less hot air in the room.

SPACE SAVING

If you are living in a compact environment, such as a studio flat, caravan or motor home, a microwave can do the job of an oven and hob while taking up a lot less space.

GETTING THE BEST FROM THIS BOOK

As this may be a whole new way of cooking for you, I have included some hints and tips on how to get the best out of this book. As with any new skill – there are tricks to the trade.

WATTAGE

Microwave wattages vary and the size of your oven cavity, whether you have a turntable or not, and whether your microwave has extra features, such as inverter technology, can all affect the timings of recipes. My timings are guidelines, and the recipes have been tested as accurately as possible in several different microwave ovens. I've given timings for 800Watt and 1000Watt machines; if yours is under 1000Watt, 900Watt for instance, follow the 800Watt timings but be prepared to add a few seconds, if necessary. (Make a note in the book for next time you cook the same recipe.) If you have a microwave with a rating of over 1000Watt, you may need to cook the recipes for slightly less time. Until you've followed a few of the recipes and got used to cooking in your own microwave oven, it's going to be a matter of checking the food a little more often. Always go for the lower timings as it's easy to add extra time but there is nothing you can do once you've overcooked something.

OUTPUT

I've tested the recipes in this book using the HIGH setting. HIGH is equivalent to 100% output. Your oven will have other settings, such as MEDIUM or DEFROST, but the output that these terms signify can vary enormously according to the make and wattage of your microwave, so I've avoided variations in order for my instructions to be as simple to follow as possible.

CONTROLS

Some very basic microwave ovens sometimes don't have an easy way of setting to cook in shorter time increments, such as 10 or even 30 seconds. These often have a dial control, which is fiddly and can be hard to set accurately. If you've tried a few of these and are enjoying the process but want more control, it's best to invest in an oven with push buttons instead.

INSTRUCTION BOOKLET

Before you start cooking any of these recipes, it is important to read and remind yourself of the manufacturer's instructions that came with your oven. You should find lots of extra tips and information pertaining to your microwave. In particular, it is important to read the section on cooking safely. There will be information on what type of containers are safe to use, and what not to put in the oven – principally metal. I have included a section on what type of dishes and bowls I find most useful (page 219) but don't forget to remind yourself of the rules of safe microwave cooking first.

DISH SIZE & SUITABILITY

In each of the recipes, I have specified a container size for the dish. It is important to follow these recommendations, as the size and shape of a container affects the cooking times. (See page 219 for the dishes I use most regularly.)

Using a wide-based dish and spreading the ingredients across the base, without letting it get too deep or piled up, will help the microwaves penetrate the food more effectively. Tall, narrow dishes don't work well for microwave cooking and should be avoided.

If you have a container and you aren't sure whether it can be used in a microwave oven, you can check very simply by filling a microwaveable jug, such as a Pyrex measuring jug, with 300ml cold water. Place it in the microwave alongside the dish that you are testing. (If the dish is large, set the jug on top or inside the empty dish.) Heat on HIGH for 1 minute. If the empty dish is suitable for microwave cooking, it will remain cool while the water in the jug will be warm. If the dish is also warming up, it means it is absorbing microwave energy and can't be used for cooking.

SPACING

When cooking individual ingredients in a microwave, such as potatoes, cupcakes or tomatoes, it's best to arrange them apart, ideally in a circle, with plenty of space in between and a gap in the middle. Long and narrow items, such as asparagus spears or thin fish fillets, can be arranged like the spokes of a wheel. This is necessary so that the microwave energy can be absorbed as efficiently as possible. The waves bounce around the oven cavity and if you take the time to arrange food correctly, it will cook more quickly and evenly.

As a rule of thumb, place thicker ends of fish fillets or chicken breasts towards the outside of the circle and the thinner ends towards the middle. Or fold the thinner ends of fish fillets, such as salmon or sole, under the thicker ends to make a more compact parcel. This will help to ensure the thinner ends don't get overcooked. Chicken breasts can also be flattened to the same thickness or turned into escalopes to encourage even cooking.

TURNING & MOVING

Many microwaves come with a turntable that rotates the food to help even cooking. If your oven doesn't have this, it's important to rearrange the food as it cooks. This may mean turning a dish a couple of times or moving items to an alternative position in the oven. Some foods, such as jacket potatoes, may need to be turned over completely during cooking for the best results and I've included this where necessary. Bear in mind that foods will be hot, so use tongs or an oven glove.

INGREDIENT DENSITY, QUANTITY & SIZE

Porous foods, such as cakes, and foods with a high water content will cook more quickly than dense, heavy foods, such as potatoes. And small amounts or pieces of an ingredient will cook or reheat more quickly than large quantities or pieces, so it's worth cutting things into smaller chunks, if possible. This way, the microwaves can penetrate the food more effectively. Try and keep the pieces an even size, though. I have taken this into account in all my recipes, and have included instructions on how to prepare each ingredient, but understanding the reasoning behind an instruction can help.

MORE THAN ONE

If you are cooking more than one of something, it will take longer to cook. It's not an exact science, though, so you can't just double the cooking time. It will depend on the size of your dishes and the density of the food, as well as its placement in the microwave. The same goes for cooking just one or two items, when the recipe calls for several. Times may have to be drastically reduced. When following the recipes in this book, it is best to be guided by the quantities and dish recommendations for the best and most reliable results.

COVERING

Microwave cooking, like any cooking, can produce splashes, so I tend to cook with the dish covered in most cases. Covering dishes also helps keep food moist and can speed up the cooking process. I prefer to cover with a microwaveable plate or plastic microwave lid, if my dish doesn't already have one. I avoid using plastic film where possible, as it generally can't be recycled. There are some good compostable films available now but a lid works well and, since food doesn't get baked onto the container in the same way as oven- or hob-cooked food, it will be easy to clean. Don't cover foods too tightly, though, or use a lid that completely seals, as this can cause it to burst. And always use an oven cloth when you are removing any lids, as hot steam can escape. If using cling film ensure it is microwave-safe, prick it a couple of times or lift it at one corner to allow the steam to escape.

STARTING TEMPERATURE

Food that's been kept in the fridge will take longer to heat up than food stored at room temperature. I've assumed that items, such as butter, cream, milk and eggs and vegetables, are cold before you start. You may need to keep a closer eye on the timings if yours are not.

PRICKING THINGS WITH SKINS

Some foods with a skin or membrane, such as sausages, apples, potatoes and eggs, should be pierced before cooking, as the water contained within will create steam that builds up and causes them to burst. (Don't microwave eggs in their shells.) Sometimes you will hear popping inside the microwave when cooking fillets of fish or whole chicken breasts. This is caused when small pockets of water expand rapidly. To avoid this, you can prick thinner areas with a cocktail stick several times before cooking. Or, if you hear popping, stop the microwave for 20–30 seconds to allow the liquid to redistribute before continuing.

STANDING & RESTING

Microwaves can easily overcook food if you aren't watching carefully, so it helps to stop the cooking process for some dishes when the food is very slightly undercooked and allow the residual heat to continue the cooking process. This is particularly important for cakes and biscuits, which can become tough or even burn if they are overcooked. (High sugar or high fat foods need to be watched carefully.) By standing the food for a few minutes at the end of the cooking time, the heat can be redistributed and become a more even temperature throughout. It's also a useful step when cooking or reheating foods with a high liquid content, such as soups or stews, although stirring will help to do this, too. If food isn't cooked properly or hot throughout after standing, return to the microwave and cook for a little longer.

TEMPERATURE

I rely on my digital food thermometer for checking the temperature of dishes especially when cooking meat and poultry, to ensure they have reached a safe eating temperature. Just like cooking on the hob or in the oven, if something reaches 75°C or over when probed in several places, any nasty bugs that might be present should have been killed. If you don't have a thermometer, you will need to check the food is piping hot throughout before serving. Cut chicken, sausages or burgers through the thickest parts to ensure there is no pinkness remaining and check that any juices run clear.

STAGED COOKING

Unlike cooking in a pan on the hob, microwaving means not watching food as it cooks but shutting the door on it while it does its thing. This means that quite often food needs to be cooked in stages. And while it can be a little frustrating at first not being able to judge visually when an ingredient is cooked and ready for the next item to be added, once you know your own microwave and get used to stopping during the cooking process, it will feel like second nature. And, if you are new to cooking, it's actually a great way of guaranteeing good results, as very little is left to chance.

Cooking in stages means taking the bowl or dish out of the microwave during the cooking process and stirring, moving or adding other ingredients. (Each recipe has clear instructions on when you need to do this.) Stirring where specified is important because food can cook at different speeds according to where it is positioned in the oven, and according to its thickness or density. When you stir or move the food, you are redistributing the ingredients, helping the microwave energy reach them and ensuring even cooking.

Don't forget that containers will get hot during the cooking process, just like they do in a conventional oven, so take care and use oven gloves when removing your dish. Also, lots of steam can be generated, so take lids off carefully for stirring, aiming the steam so that it blows away from you.

STAGES MIGHT INCLUDE:

- Melting butter
- Softening vegetables
- Cooking meats
- Adding new ingredients
- Changing the position of ingredients
- Turning ingredients over
- Stirring sauces
- Whisking to prevent lumps

BREAKFASTS & BRUCNH

Microwave Porridge

Serves 1
Ready in under 5 mins

35g rolled porridge oats (not jumbo)
225ml milk, plus a little extra
    to serve

This is the easiest way to cook porridge. Serve it just as it is, or top with golden syrup, brown sugar, honey, fruit, yoghurt or a drizzle of cold milk. You can stir in a few chopped nuts, some sliced banana or grated chocolate and cook it for an extra 20–30 secs for an extra-indulgent breakfast.

Mix the oats with the milk in a medium microwaveable bowl – it will need to be large enough for the porridge to rise up as it boils. Cook, without covering, on HIGH for 2 mins 30 secs (1000W) or 3 mins (800W), stirring after 2 mins.

Stir and pour carefully into a large cereal bowl. Top with golden syrup, brown sugar, honey or fruit compote (page 21) and a drizzle of cold milk, if you like.

Micro-tip —— You can cook it in the bowl you wish to eat it from, if you like, but it will need to be microwaveable and able to hold at least 800ml liquid.

Warm Berry Compote

Serves 2
Ready in under 5 mins

150g frozen fruit (such as mixed
berries, cherries or mango
pieces)
40g caster sugar or 4 tbsp maple
syrup, or to taste

A super-quick compote to serve with pancakes, toasted waffles
or Greek yoghurt and granola. It's also delicious spooned over
ice cream.

Put the frozen fruit and sugar or maple syrup in a medium
microwaveable bowl. Cover and cook on HIGH for 2 mins (1000W),
2 mins 30 secs (800W), or until the fruit is hot and softened enough
to create juicy syrup.

Serve the warm compote with pancakes, waffles or yoghurt, if eating for
breakfast, or whipped cream, if having as dessert.

Micro-tips —— Fruit such as
mango will release less juice, so add
a splash of orange juice or a little extra
sugar, if you like a lot of syrup.

Swap frozen for fresh berries, if you
like, and reduce the cooking time by
a few secs.

Breakfast Muffins

Makes 4
Ready in under 15 mins

50g butter, cubed

50g soft dark brown sugar

1 medium egg

50g Greek-style yoghurt

50g self-raising flour

½ tsp baking powder

½ tsp ground cinnamon

50g granola, any large clumps
    broken up

50g fresh blueberries

15g mixed seeds, to decorate

A breakfast bowl of yoghurt, granola and fresh blueberries turned into light and fluffy muffins. Making just four at a time, instead of baking a tray of 12 in the oven, is both quick and easy, but you could double or triple the quantities and cook them in batches, if you prefer.

Line four medium ramekins (arond 175ml each) with paper muffin or cupcake cases.

Put the butter in a large microwaveable mixing bowl. Cover and cook on HIGH for 20 secs (1000W), 30 secs (800W), or until melted.

Add the sugar, egg and yoghurt to the melted butter and whisk until thoroughly combined. Add the flour, baking powder and cinnamon and beat until smooth.

Stir in the granola and blueberries, and divide the batter between the prepared ramekins. Don't overfill the ramekins; the muffin batter should rise roughly halfway up the cases.

Sprinkle with the seeds and place the ramekins in a circle straight onto the turntable or base of the microwave oven, leaving plenty of space in between each one. Cook uncovered on HIGH for 3 mins 30 secs (1000W), 4 mins 30 secs (800W), or until risen and just firm. If the mixture appears uncooked, continue cooking in 20 sec increments until done. The muffins will continue cooking for a short while once out of the microwave, so if they look just a little damp around the sides, that's fine.

Leave to stand for 5 mins in the microwave before turning out. Serve warm or cool.

Micro-tip —— The exact timings will depend on the size of your ramekins and how much the mixture can spread. If you don't have any ramekins, you can place the cases in microwaveable cups or mugs instead.

Poached Egg

Serves 1
Ready in under 3 mins

200ml just-boiled water from
a kettle
1 medium egg, fridge cold

With a firm white and a deliciously runny yolk, these are best served on hot buttered toast, English muffins or bagels. Top with smoked salmon or sliced ham and Hollandaise Sauce (page 203) for an extra decadent brunch. If you've avoided cooking poached eggs in the past because of disastrous results, this is the way to do it! Use very fresh medium eggs for the best results.

Pour the just-boiled water into a medium microwaveable bowl (see Micro-tip). Crack the egg carefully into the centre.

Cook without covering on HIGH for about 40 secs (1000W or 800W – the cooking time won't vary much between wattages).

Leave to stand for 60 secs before lifting out of the water with a slotted spoon and draining.

Micro-tips —— Use a 1-litre
bowl with a diameter at the top of 17cm for the best results – it's a pretty standard size. A large cereal bowl could work, but you may need to have a couple of goes until the cooking time is perfect. If serving more than one egg, it's best to cook them separately.

Pour the hot water straight from the kettle into the bowl and weigh the water on electric scales as accurately as you can. It might seem pedantic but the right amount of water will make all the difference to the results.

Scrambled Eggs

Serves 1
Ready in under 5 mins

15g butter (around 1 tbsp)
2 medium or large eggs

My method for cooking scrambled eggs in the microwave gives deliciously creamy results and produces less washing up than the standard method. You do need to whisk a couple of times as they cook, but I promise you it's worth it!

Put the butter into a medium microwaveable mixing bowl and cook uncovered on HIGH for 15 secs (1000W), 20 secs (800W), or until melted.

Break the eggs into the bowl and whisk thoroughly. (As egg white and yolk set at different temperatures, it's important to beat well to avoid uneven cooking.) Season with salt and ground black pepper.

Cook uncovered on HIGH for 1 min (1000W) or 1 min 20 secs (800W), removing the bowl from the microwave and whisking every 30 secs until softly set. The egg will start setting around the sides before the centre, which is why it is important to whisk regularly as it cooks.

Micro-tips —— Medium or
large eggs can be used for this recipe as the timings won't vary too much. If not using fridge-cold eggs, though, you will need to reduce the cooking time slightly.

If cooking for more than one person, you will need to increase the cooking time.

Cream of Tomato Soup

Serves 2
Ready in under 15 mins

350g fresh ripe tomatoes, roughly
    chopped
1 garlic clove, peeled and crushed
1 tbsp tomato purée
1 tbsp extra-virgin olive oil
1 tsp caster sugar
250ml hot vegetable stock
    (made using ½ stock cube)
2 tbsp double or single cream,
    plus extra to serve

An utterly delicious soup that makes the most of fresh tomatoes and is almost as easy as opening a can. Use any kind or tomatoes – those soft ones lurking at the back of the fridge that aren't quite good enough for a salad will shine here. If you don't want to use cream, simply leave it out or add a few fresh basil leaves before blitzing, for a fresh-tasting alternative.

Put the tomatoes in a large microwaveable bowl or jug. It will need to hold at least 2 litres. Cover and cook on HIGH for 4 mins (1000W) or 5 mins (800W), until well softened, stirring halfway.

Stir in the garlic, tomato purée, oil and sugar. Season with salt and ground black pepper, cover and cook on HIGH for 1 min (1000W) or 1 min 10 secs (800W).

Stir in the hot stock, cover and cook on HIGH for 2 mins (1000W) or 2 mins 30 secs (800W).

Blitz with a stick blender until as smooth as possible.

Stir in the cream, check the seasoning and serve drizzled with a little extra cream.

Pea and Watercress Soup

Serves 2–3
Ready in under 15 mins

1 tbsp sunflower or vegetable oil

25g butter, cubed

½ medium onion, peeled and finely
chopped

300g frozen peas

80g watercress or other salad leaves

10 fresh mint leaves or ½ tsp dried
mint

300ml hot vegetable or chicken
stock (made with ½ stock cube)

drizzle of cream, to serve (optional)

When you fancy a quick bowl of home-made soup, reach for this recipe. Made with a handful of ingredients, it's great for using up bags of salad leaves that you might have knocking about in the fridge.

Mix the oil, butter, onion and a generous grinding of black pepper in a large microwaveable bowl or casserole. Cover and cook on HIGH for 3 mins (1000W), 3 mins 40 secs (800W), or until the onion is softened.

Stir in the peas, watercress or other salad leaves and mint. Pour in the stock, cover and cook on HIGH for 4 mins (1000W) or 5 mins (800W), stirring halfway.

Blitz with a stick blender until as smooth as possible, then add a little extra seasoning, if needed. (You can also leave the soup to cool for a few minutes, then blitz in a food processor.)

Return to the microwave, cover and cook on HIGH for 2 mins (1000W) or 2 mins 30 secs (800W), or until hot.

Delicious hot or cold, topped with a drizzle of cream, if you like.

So-simple Mushroom Soup

Serves 2
Ready in under 12 mins

250g fresh mushrooms (any kind),
    thinly sliced
25g butter, cubed
1 small garlic clove, peeled and
    crushed
1 tbsp plain flour
100ml hot vegetable stock (made
    with ½ stock cube)
100ml milk (ideally whole milk)
2–3 tbsp single or double cream, or
    crème fraiche, plus extra to serve
    (optional)
freshly chopped parsley or chives,
    to serve (optional)

A great way to use up mushrooms when they are on offer, or when you have a few knocking around in your fridge. It's incredibly quick and easy. It's particularly delicious with a little added cream, but lovely without, too.

Put the mushrooms and butter in a large microwaveable bowl and season with salt and ground black pepper. Cover and cook on HIGH for 4 mins (1000W) or 5 mins (800W), stirring halfway.

Stir in the garlic and flour, cover and cook on HIGH for 30 secs (1000W) or 40 secs (800W).

Stir in the stock and milk, cover and cook on HIGH for 2 mins (1000W) or 2 mins 30 secs (800W), or until hot.

Add the cream or crème fraiche, if using, and blitz with a stick blender until smooth. Adjust the seasoning to taste.

Serve with a drizzle more cream, a sprinkling of fresh herbs, if you like, and lots of warm crusty bread.

Cheesy Jacket Potatoes

Serves 2–4
Ready in under 20 mins

3 medium-large potatoes
(preferably Maris Piper; each
around 250g)
knob of butter (around 20g)
3 tbsp milk or cream
65g mature Cheddar (or other
cheese), coarsely grated
finely sliced spring onions or chives,
to serve (optional)

It's easy to make a simple jacket spud into something much more delicious with a microwave. And instead of taking over an hour in the oven, these are ready in under 20 mins. Makes two generous portions or four smaller servings.

Prick the potatoes 3–4 times all over with a fork. Place on a microwaveable plate lined with plain, microwave-safe kitchen paper (make sure it isn't recycled – see page 221). Cook uncovered on HIGH for 12 mins (1000W) or 15 mins (800W), turning every 4–5 mins. They should feel soft if you squeeze them. If there are hard patches, turn them over again and cook for a further 1–2 mins.

Leave to stand for 2–3 mins. (If you like, you can serve the potatoes just as they are now.)

Cut the potatoes in half, taking care as they will be hot. Use a teaspoon to scoop out most of the potato into a bowl, leaving a thin layer of potato around the sides. Mash the potato in the bowl with the butter and milk or cream until light and fluffy. Season with salt and ground black pepper, then stir in half the cheese.

Put the potato skins, cut side up, back on the microwaveable plate. Spoon the cheesy mash into the potato skins and sprinkle with the remaining cheese. Cook uncovered on HIGH for 2 mins (1000W), 2 mins 30 secs (800W), or until the cheese has melted and the potatoes are hot.

Sprinkle with finely sliced spring onion or chives to serve, if using.

Micro-tip —— You can serve the potatoes plain, without the cheese, or you could stir some canned tuna and sweetcorn into the mash instead of cheese. You could also mash the potato simply with a little butter and top with soured cream and chives. Add a sprinkling of Topping Mix (page 211) before returning the stuffed potatoes to the microwave.

Loaded Nachos

Serves 3–4
Ready in under 5 mins

125g lightly salted tortilla chips
100g mature Cheddar, coarsely
    grated
100g tomato salsa, from a jar
75g sliced jalapeño chillies, from a
    jar, well drained
75g soured cream or half-fat crème
    fraiche
freshly chopped coriander, to serve
    (optional)

I often knock nachos together as an easy snack for friends. The quantities don't have to be exact, so you'll be able to make them without the recipe in no time.

Put roughly a third of the tortilla chips in a large, shallow microwaveable bowl and sprinkle with roughly a third of the cheese. Spoon over a third of the salsa.

Repeat the layers twice more, ending with the cheese and salsa. You don't need to be too exact about it, you just want to make sure a little cheese and salsa ends up on each tortilla chip. Cook on HIGH for 2 mins (1000W), 2 mins 30 secs (800W), or until the cheese has melted.

Scatter with the jalapeños and top with the soured cream or crème fraiche and a scattering of fresh coriander, if using, to serve.

'Baked' Camembert

Serves 4
Ready in under 5 mins

250g round Camembert
25g pecan or walnut halves, roughly
    chopped
2 tbsp runny honey
fresh thyme leaves, to serve
    (optional)

You'll wonder why you ever bothered baking Camembert in the oven when you discover how simple and quick it is in the microwave. Serve with fresh fruit or vegetable sticks and crackers or crusty bread for dipping.

Take the Camembert out of its box and remove the wrapping. Place on a board and carefully cut the top rind off and discard.

Put the cheese, cut side up, in the centre of a microwaveable plate. Scatter the nuts on the cheese and drizzle with the honey. Season with lots of ground black pepper. Cook on HIGH for 50 secs (1000W), 1 min (800W), or until the cheese is hot and just melted. It will continue melting for a few mins after you remove it from the microwave.

Scatter over the thyme, if using, to serve.

Microwave Pizzas

Makes 2
Ready in under 10 mins

2 white or wholemeal pitta breads

3 tbsp tomato purée

¼ tsp dried oregano

50g ready-grated mozzarella and
    Cheddar

a few toppings (such as salami,
    chorizo or ham, olives, thinly
    sliced mushrooms, roasted
    pepper strips, tomatoes, goat's
    cheese, pesto or rocket)

extra-virgin olive oil, to serve

small handful of fresh herbs, to
    serve (optional)

Super-fast and convenient, these pizzas have a fluffy base and a rich, cheesy top. Add any of your favourite toppings or serve simply as a margherita. You can even use the pitta bread straight from the freezer – just increase the cooking time a little.

Put the pitta breads on two microwaveable plates. Spread each one with some tomato purée, then sprinkle with a little of the oregano and the grated cheese.

Finish with a few of your favourite toppings and season with a little more oregano and lots of ground black pepper. Cook one at a time, uncovered, on HIGH for 50–60 secs (1000W), 60–70 secs (800W), or until the cheese has melted and the toppings are hot. The exact timings will depend on the kind of toppings you have used.

Drizzle with a little extra-virgin olive oil and sprinkle with fresh herbs, if using, to serve.

Micro-tip —— Ready-grated
mixed mozzarella and Cheddar comes in bags and is great for making pizzas. If you can't get hold of any, use grated Cheddar on the pizzas instead.

Warm Goat's Cheese Salad

Serves 1
Ready in under 5 mins

For the salad

large handful of mixed salad
    leaves (around 40g)
6 cherry tomatoes, halved
5 heaped tsp soft goat's cheese
5 ready-made crostini, from a
    packet

For the dressing

2 tbsp extra-virgin olive oil
2 tsp balsamic vinegar
½ tsp caster sugar

Using your microwave means you can make a quick and healthy lunch of creamy goat's cheese on crispy crostini in just 5 mins. Double up the ingredients to serve two, and you could add wedges of cooked beetroot and a handful of roughly chopped toasted hazelnuts to the salad, if you like.

Place the salad leaves in a shallow bowl and scatter the tomatoes on top.

Spread the goat's cheese over the crostini and place spaced apart on a microwaveable plate. Cook uncovered on HIGH for 20 secs (1000W), 30 secs (800W), or until hot. Arrange the crostini on top of the salad.

Whisk the dressing ingredients together in a small microwaveable bowl. Season with salt and ground black pepper and cook uncovered on HIGH for 20 secs – do not allow to overheat.

Drizzle the warm dressing over the salad and serve.

Micro-tip —— You will find ready-made crostini in supermarkets in the savoury biscuit section. But you can also make your own by toasting thin slices of French bread until crisp.

CHICKEN & TURKEY

Pizza Chicken

Serves 1
Ready in under 10 mins

1 skinless, boneless chicken breast
      (around 175g)
1 tbsp tomato purée
good pinch of dried oregano or
      dried Italian herbs
15g ready-grated mozzarella and
      Cheddar, or Cheddar, coarsely
      grated
extra-virgin olive oil and fresh basil,
      to serve (optional)

Probably the fastest and most succulent chicken you will ever taste! I've written the recipe for one, but you could double, triple or quadruple the quantities – so long as you cook them one at a time. Serve hot or cold.

Place the chicken breast on a board between two sheets of non-stick baking paper. Use the base of a saucepan to beat the chicken, starting at the thickest end, until it is around 1.5cm all over. Prick all the way around the edges of the breast (see tip on page 12).

Place the chicken on a microwaveable plate and season with salt and ground black pepper. Spread the tomato purée on the chicken, sprinkle with the herbs and top with the cheese. Finish with a little more of the herbs and a grinding of black pepper.

Cover with a microwave lid or upturned microwaveable bowl and cook on HIGH for 2 mins (1000W) or 2 mins 30 secs (800W).

Leave to stand for 1 min, then cook on HIGH for 1 min (1000W), 1 min 10 secs (800W), or until the chicken is cooked through and the cheese has melted. (If using a digital food thermometer to check the chicken, it should read over 75°C.)

Leave to stand, covered, for 5 mins. Discard any cooking juices that have collected under the chicken.

Drizzle with a little olive oil and sprinkle with fresh basil, if using, to serve.

Micro-tip —— Chicken
breast sizes can vary enormously. Be prepared to reduce or increase the cooking time.

Some chicken may 'pop' as it cooks. If this starts to happen, stop cooking for a few secs to allow the heat to redistribute before continuing.

'Roast' Chicken in 40 Minutes

Serves 4
Ready in under 40 mins

1 small whole chicken (no bigger
    than 1.3kg)
2 bay leaves (optional)
2 tbsp sunflower or vegetable oil
2 tsp ground paprika (not smoked)
1 chicken stock cube
1 tsp dried parsley
½ tsp dried thyme

Wonderful served hot with gravy and all the trimmings, or cold for salads and sandwiches. This recipe cooks a succulent rotisserie-style chicken in around 40 mins.

Remove any trussing string and place the bay leaves, if using, inside the chicken. You can retie the chicken legs loosely with kitchen string, if you like. Prick the bird 12–15 times all over with a cocktail stick or the tip of a wooden skewer. Put the chicken breast-side down on a microwaveable plate and cook on HIGH for 3 mins (1000W) or 3 mins 40 secs (800W).

Meanwhile, in a small bowl, mix 1 tbsp of the oil with the paprika and stock cube, pressing and crushing the stock cube until it blends to a paste. Stir in the remaining oil.

Transfer the chicken to a wide-based microwaveable dish. Brush the paste all over the chicken and season with ground black pepper. Sprinkle with the dried herbs and cover the chicken with a microwaveable roasting bag (see Micro-tip). Cook on HIGH for 15 mins (1000W) or 19 mins (800W).

Test the temperature through the thickest part of the breast and thigh using a digital food thermometer – it should reach 70°C or more. Check carefully close to the breast bone, as this part takes the longest to cook. If not, return to the microwave and cook for a few mins more.

Cover with a clean tea towel without removing the bag and leave to rest for 15 mins. The temperature inside the chicken should continue rising as it rests. Ensure it reaches 75°C or more and is cooked through before serving.

Warm the cooking juices and drizzle over the chicken to serve, or use to make a thicker gravy.

Micro-tips — Cut one long side of a roasting bag and open out. Tent the chicken with the bag, tucking in around the sides.

If you don't have a turntable in your microwave, turn the dish every 5 mins.

One-pot Spicy Chicken and Rice

Serves 4
Ready in under 20 mins

1 tbsp sunflower or vegetable oil

1 medium onion, peeled and finely chopped

2 large peppers (any colour), deseeded and cut into roughly 2cm chunks

1½ tsp Cajun seasoning

2 boneless, skinless chicken breasts (around 350g total weight), cut widthways into 1cm thin slices

100g chorizo, thinly sliced

2 garlic cloves, peeled and crushed

200g basmati rice

350ml hot chicken stock (made with 1 stock cube)

100g frozen peas, thawed

A quick, colourful family supper made in one dish and ready in under 20 mins. If you don't have any Cajun seasoning, you can use any other dried spice mix – piri piri, fajita and Moroccan should all work well. Or simply add 1 tsp hot smoked paprika.

Mix the oil, onion, peppers, Cajun seasoning and a few twists of ground black pepper in a large microwaveable casserole dish or wide-based bowl (it will need to hold at least 2.5 litres). Cover and cook on HIGH for 4 mins (1000W) or 5 mins (800W), stirring halfway.

Stir in the chicken, chorizo and garlic. Cover and cook on HIGH for 2 mins (1000W) or 2 mins 30 secs (800W).

Stir in the rice and hot stock, making sure all the rice is submerged under the liquid. Cover with a lid or film and cook on HIGH for 5 mins (1000W and 800W), stirring halfway.

Stir in the peas and cook on HIGH for 5 mins (1000W and 800W), or until the rice is tender and most of the liquid has been absorbed.

Leave to stand for 5 mins before serving.

Micro-tips —— You can use 4 boneless, skinless chicken thigh fillets (around 400g total weight), cut into 2–3cm pieces instead of the breast, if you like.

To thaw the peas, put them in a bowl, cover with just-boiled water, then drain.

Easy Chicken Casserole

Serves 4
Ready in under 35 mins

A simple chicken casserole that's ready in just 35 mins and makes a brilliant midweek family meal. Serve with mashed or boiled potatoes and some freshly cooked green veg.

6 boneless, skinless chicken thighs (around 600g total weight), trimmed of fat and quartered

1 tbsp sunflower or vegetable oil

1 medium onion, peeled and thinly sliced

3–4 medium carrots (around 300g), peeled and cut into roughly 5mm slices

¼ tsp dried thyme or 2 tsp fresh thyme leaves

3 rashers smoked back bacon, cut into roughly 1.5cm slices

1 medium leek (around 175g), trimmed and cut into roughly 1cm slices

2 tbsp cornflour mixed with 2 tbsp cold water

300ml hot chicken stock (made with 1 cube)

1 tbsp wholegrain or Dijon mustard

2 tbsp double or single cream, or crème fraiche (optional)

Place the chicken in a large microwaveable casserole or wide-based bowl (see Micro-tip). Add the oil, onion, carrots, thyme, a little salt and lots of ground black pepper and toss well together. Cover and cook on HIGH for 5 mins (1000W) or 6 mins 10 secs (800W).

Add the bacon and leek and stir well. Cover and cook on HIGH for 7 mins (1000W), 8 mins 40 secs (800W), or until the carrots are softened, stirring halfway.

Stir the cornflour mixture into the hot stock, then add the mustard and stir well.

Pour the hot stock mixture into the chicken and vegetables, stir then cover and cook on HIGH for 5 mins (1000W), 6 mins 10 secs (800W), or until the sauce is thickened and bubbling.

Leave to stand for 5 mins.

Stir in the cream or crème fraiche, if using, and serve.

Micro-tip — Choose a deepish dish with a nice wide base. If your dish can hold around 2.5 litres of water, it is just the right size.

Paprika Chicken

Serves 5
Ready in under 35 mins, plus standing

2 tbsp sunflower or vegetable oil

1 medium onion, peeled and thinly sliced

2 garlic cloves, peeled and crushed

3 peppers (any colour), deseeded and cut into roughly 3cm chunks

1–2 tsp hot smoked paprika

1 tsp dried mixed herbs

1½ tbsp plain flour (around 20g)

1 × 400g can chopped tomatoes

2 tbsp tomato purée

150ml hot chicken stock (made with 1 stock cube)

75ml white wine (or more chicken stock)

3–4 boneless, skinless chicken breasts (around 600g), trimmed and cut into roughly 3cm chunks

freshly chopped parsley and soured cream, to serve (optional)

A warming, hearty chicken dish with a rich, spiced tomato sauce. Perfect for a simple midweek supper. Serve with rice, jacket or mashed potatoes, and top with lots of soured cream or crème fraîche.

Put the oil, onion, garlic, peppers, paprika, herbs, a little salt and lots of ground black pepper in a large, wide-based microwaveable dish or casserole (it will need to hold at least 2.5 litres) and stir well.

Cover and cook on HIGH for 6 mins (1000W) or 7 mins 30 secs (800W), stirring halfway.

Sprinkle the flour over the vegetables and toss everything together. Add the canned tomatoes, tomato purée, stock and wine, if using. Stir well, then cover and cook on HIGH for 4 mins (1000W) or 5 mins (800W).

Put the chicken in a bowl and toss with a little salt and lots of ground black pepper. Stir the chicken into the tomato sauce, cover and cook on HIGH for 12 mins (1000W), 15 mins (800W), or until the chicken is thoroughly cooked, stirring three times.

Stand for 5 mins before serving topped with a scattering of parsley and some soured cream, if you like.

Micro-tip —— You can reduce the hot smoked paprika or use plain paprika, if you like your food less spicy.

Barbecue-Style Chicken

Serves 4–5
Ready in under 30 mins

14–16 chicken mini fillets (around 640g total weight), cut off the white part of each mini fillet
1 tbsp sunflower or vegetable oil
½ tsp hot smoked paprika

For the sauce
75g tomato ketchup
3 tbsp runny honey
2 tbsp Worcestershire sauce
1 tsp hot smoked paprika
1 garlic clove, peeled and crushed

Piled into warm wraps or soft buns and served with lashings of soured cream or yoghurt, alongside salad and lime wedges, this tangy chicken is sure to become a family favourite. Any leftovers will keep well in the fridge for a couple of days and can be served cold as well as hot.

Toss the chicken with the oil, paprika and a good pinch of salt and lots of ground black pepper. Arrange on two large microwaveable plates, cover and cook one plate at a time on HIGH for 3 mins (1000W) or 3 mins 40 secs (800W), turning and repositioning the fillets on the plates halfway. If the chicken is not cooked after this time, turn again and return to the microwave for 20–30 secs, or until cooked through. Set aside.

To make the sauce, mix the ketchup, honey, Worcestershire sauce, paprika, garlic and a good pinch of salt and lots of ground black pepper in a large microwaveable dish. Cover and cook on HIGH for 2 mins (1000W) or 2 mins 30 secs (800W).

Drain the chicken pieces and add to the sauce. Stir until well coated then return to the microwave and cook, uncovered, on HIGH for 4 mins (1000W) or 5 mins (800W), stirring halfway, until hot.

Leave to stand for 5 mins before serving the chicken whole or shredding it by pulling apart with two forks.

Chicken and Mushroom Risotto

Serves 3–4
Ready in under 35 mins

10g dried mushrooms (any kind), broken into small pieces

250ml just-boiled water, from a kettle

1 medium onion, peeled and finely chopped

200g small mushrooms (preferably chestnut), sliced or quartered

2 garlic cloves, peeled and very thinly sliced

1 tbsp sunflower or vegetable oil

200g risotto rice (such as Arborio)

225ml hot chicken stock (made with 1 stock cube)

75ml white wine (or extra stock)

2–3 boneless, skinless chicken breasts (around 400g total weight), cut widthways into 5mm thin slices

50g Parmesan or other hard cheese, finely grated, plus extra to serve

freshly chopped parsley, to serve (optional)

This full-flavoured risotto is quick to assemble and can be left to cook in the microwave, so you don't need to stand stirring it for ages. The dried mushrooms give it a rich, luxurious taste and can be found in larger supermarkets. If you don't have any handy, leave them out and add an extra 250ml stock.

Put the dried mushrooms in a measuring jug and add the just-boiled water. Leave to stand for roughly 10 mins, until softened.

Put the onion, fresh mushrooms and garlic in a large microwaveable bowl or casserole – it will need to be large enough to hold at least 2.5 litres liquid. Add the oil, season with salt and lots of ground black pepper and toss together well. Cover and cook on HIGH for 5 mins (1000W) or 6 mins 10 secs (800W), until softened, stirring halfway.

Add the dried mushrooms and their soaking liquor to the fresh mushrooms with the rice, hot stock and wine, if using, and stir well. Cover and cook on HIGH for 5 mins (1000W) or 6 mins 10 secs (800W).

Stir in the chicken, cover and cook on HIGH for 10 mins (1000W) or 12 mins 30 secs (800W), stirring halfway. By this point, the rice should be tender and most of the liquid absorbed, but timings may vary according to the shape of your dish, so add 1–2 mins, if needed.

Stir in the grated cheese and adjust the seasoning to taste. Serve with an extra sprinkling of cheese and some freshly chopped parsley, if you like.

Micro-tip —— For a vegetarian version, leave out the chicken, increase the fresh mushrooms and swap the chicken stock for vegetable stock.

Thai Chicken Coconut Curry

Serves 3
Ready in under 20 mins

6 spring onions, trimmed and sliced

1 red pepper, deseeded and thinly
sliced

25g fresh root ginger, peeled and
finely grated

3 tbsp good-quality Thai red or
green curry paste (around 45g)

1 × 400ml can coconut milk

175g mixed mangetout or sugar
snap peas and baby corn, halved
diagonally

2 boneless, skinless chicken breasts
(around 350g total weight), cut
widthways into 5mm thin slices

small bunch of fresh coriander
(around 15g), roughly chopped,
plus extra to serve

A fool-proof Thai-style coconut curry that's a doddle to prepare.
You can add any vegetables you like – sliced peppers and fine
green beans work well – just keep the weight roughly the same.
Feel free to add a few makrut lime leaves or sliced fresh red chillies,
if you have some handy. Serve with rice or noodles.

Mix the spring onions, red pepper, ginger and curry paste in a large
microwaveable casserole or wide-based bowl – it will need to hold
at least 2.5 litres liquid. Stir lightly. Cover and cook on HIGH for 3 mins
(1000W) or 3 mins 40 secs (800W).

Stir in the coconut milk, mangetout or sugar snap peas and baby corn,
cover and cook on HIGH for 4 mins (1000W) or 5 mins (800W).

Stir in the sliced chicken and chopped coriander, cover and cook on
HIGH for 3 mins (1000W) or 3 mins 40 secs (800W).

Stir well, cover and cook on HIGH for a final 2 mins (1000W), 2 mins 30
secs (800W), or until the chicken is cooked through. Take care as you
remove the dish from the oven as the sauce will be very hot.

Leave to stand for 5 mins.

Add seasoning to taste and scatter with extra coriander, if using,
to serve.

Micro-tip —— You can use
cooked or raw prawns or tofu instead
of chicken, if you like. Add before the
final 2 mins (1000W) or 2 mins 30
secs (800W) of cooking time, and
make sure they are thoroughly hot
before serving.

Butter Chicken Curry

Serves 2–4
Ready in under 25 mins

Probably the quickest, most delicious, creamy chicken curry you'll ever make. It serves two people very generously, three well and four if you serve it alongside other curries or side dishes – you choose!

25g butter, cubed

20g fresh root ginger, peeled
  and finely grated

3 large garlic cloves, peeled
  and finely grated

3 tsp medium curry powder

8 green cardamom pods, seeds
  crushed, or ½ tsp ground
  cardamom

¼ tsp ground turmeric

1 tbsp caster sugar

2 tbsp tomato purée

2–3 boneless, skinless chicken
  breasts (around 400g total
  weight), cut into roughly
  3cm chunks

100ml double cream

Put the butter in a wide-based microwaveable dish or casserole. Add the ginger and garlic and microwave uncovered on HIGH for 1 min (1000W) or 1 min 10 secs (800W), stirring halfway, until the butter melts and the garlic and ginger soften.

Stir in the curry powder, cardamom seeds, turmeric, sugar, tomato purée and 50ml water. Add the chicken pieces, season well with salt and ground black pepper, and stir to coat with the spice mixture. Cover and cook on HIGH for 3 mins (1000W) or 3 mins 40 secs (800W).

Stir in most of the cream, saving some to drizzle. Cover and cook on HIGH for a final 3 mins (1000W), 3 mins 40 secs (800W), or until the sauce is hot and bubbling, and the chicken pieces are cooked through.

Leave to stand for 5 mins. Adjust the seasoning to taste, drizzle with the reserved cream and serve with rice or flat breads.

Micro-tip —— You can use halved chicken mini fillets for this dish.

Creamy Tarragon Chicken

Serves 2–3
Ready in under 15 mins

350–400g chicken mini fillets

½ tsp ground paprika

½ tsp ground turmeric

¼ tsp dried thyme

2 tbsp white wine

1½ tbsp finely chopped fresh
   tarragon, plus extra to serve, or
   1½ tsp dried tarragon

150ml hot chicken stock (made with
   ½ stock cube)

100ml double cream

4 tsp cornflour mixed with 2 tbsp
   cold water

Mini chicken fillets cook beautifully in the microwave, remaining tender and succulent. Teamed with a creamy tarragon sauce, this quick dish is bound to become a favourite. Serve with rice or potatoes.

Snip the white part out of each mini fillet with kitchen scissors or a small knife.

Mix the paprika, turmeric and thyme in a bowl with a good pinch of salt and lots of ground black pepper. Toss the chicken in the seasoning mix until lightly coated.

Arrange the chicken in a single layer in a wide-based, shallow microwaveable dish. Cover and cook on HIGH for 3 mins (1000W) or 3 mins 40 secs (800W), turning and repositioning the chicken in the dish halfway. If the chicken isn't fully cooked after this time, return to the microwave for 30–40 secs, or until cooked through. Set aside.

Put the wine and tarragon in a large microwaveable bowl and cook uncovered on HIGH for 30 secs (1000W) or 40 secs (800W).

Stir in the chicken stock, cream and cornflour mixture, and season with ground black pepper. Cover and cook on HIGH for 2 mins (1000W), 2 mins 30 secs (800W), or until the sauce thickens. Stir well and check the seasoning.

Pour the sauce over the chicken and sprinkle with more fresh tarragon, if you like. Cover and cook on HIGH for 2 mins 30 secs (1000W), 3 mins 10 secs (800W), or until the chicken is hot and the sauce is bubbling.

Chicken, Mushroom and Bacon Pie

Serves 4
Ready in under 35 mins

A creamy chicken pie cooked in the microwave is perfectly possible, if you top it with crunchy ready-made croutons instead of pastry.

2 boneless, skinless chicken breasts (around 350g total weight)

½ tsp dried mixed herbs

½ medium onion, peeled and finely chopped

200g small chestnut mushrooms, halved or sliced

2 thick rashers smoked bacon, cut into roughly 1.5cm slices

25g butter, cubed

300ml hot chicken stock (made with ½ stock cube)

2 tbsp cornflour mixed with 2 tbsp cold water

3 tbsp double or single cream, or crème fraiche

For the topping
80–100g ready-made croutons

25g Cheddar, finely grated (optional)

fresh chopped parsley, to serve (optional)

Put the chicken breasts on a microwaveable plate and season with a little salt and lots of ground black pepper. Prick all around the sides of the breasts with a cocktail stick (page 12). Sprinkle with half of the dried herbs, cover and cook on HIGH for 2 mins (1000W) or 2 mins 30 secs (800W).

Turn the chicken over and cook on HIGH for a futher 2 mins (1000W), 2 mins 30 secs (800W), or until the chicken is cooked through. Leave to stand.

Put the onion, mushrooms, bacon and remaining herbs in a roughly 1.5 litre microwaveable pie dish. Dot with the butter, then cover and cook on HIGH for 6 mins (1000W), 7 mins 30 secs (800W), or until the onion is very soft, stirring halfway.

Stir in the stock and the cornflour mixture. Cover and cook on HIGH for 3 mins (1000W), 3 mins 40 secs (800W), or until the sauce is thickened. Stir in the cream.

Cut the chicken into bite-sized pieces and stir into the sauce, along with any resting juices.

Sprinkle with the croutons and cheese, if using, and season with a little ground black pepper. Cook uncovered on HIGH for 2 mins (1000W), 2 mins 30 secs (800W), or until the chicken is hot and the cheese, if using, is melted.

Scatter with freshly chopped parsley, if using, and serve.

Micro-tip —— Serve the pie as soon as it is made and before the croutons have a chance to soften. You can find ready-made croutons in most supermarkets.

Turkey Enchiladas

Makes 8
Ready in under 30 mins

250g turkey thigh mince

1 medium onion, peeled and finely chopped

1 red pepper, deseeded and diced

2 tsp ground cumin

2 tsp ground coriander

1 × 400g can black beans or kidney beans, drained and rinsed

1 × 195g can sweetcorn, drained

15g fresh coriander, leaves roughly chopped, plus extra to serve (optional)

8 regular flour tortillas, warmed

200g mature Cheddar, coarsely grated

For the sauce
300g passata

4 tsp chipotle paste, from a jar

A Tex-Mex favourite – I like using turkey but any minced meat would work well. You can prep the turkey filling ahead, if you like, and pop the filled enchiladas in the microwave just before serving – very handy if you have family eating at different times. Serve with jalapeños, soured cream, lime wedges and avocado, if you like.

Put the mince, onion, pepper, ground cumin, ground coriander, a good pinch of salt and lots of ground black pepper in a large, wide-based microwaveable dish. Using your hands, combine all the ingredients together really well, so the onion is evenly dispersed.

Cover and cook on HIGH for 4 mins (1000W) or 5 mins (800W).

Break up the meat with two wooden spatulas or spoons using a vertical chopping action (see tip on page 224). Cover and cook on HIGH for 2 mins (1000W) or 2 mins 30 secs (800W).

Break up the meat thoroughly once more, then stir in the beans, sweetcorn and fresh coriander, if using.

To make the sauce, mix the tomato passata and chipotle paste in a small bowl until well combined.

Stir 5 tbsp of the sauce into the turkey mixture, then spoon two heaped serving spoons of the mince down the centre of a tortilla. Top with a small handful of cheese, then roll up.

Put the enchilada on a plate and spoon 2 tbsp of the sauce over the top. Sprinkle with a little more cheese, then cook uncovered on HIGH for 1 min (1000W), 1 min 10 secs (800W), or until the cheese melts and the filling is hot. Repeat with the remaining mince and tortillas.

Sprinkle with more fresh coriander, if using, to serve.

Micro-tip — If you are cooking two enchiladas on one plate, you will need to increase the cooking time by roughly 30 secs.

LAMB, BEEF & PORK

Easy Meatballs

Serves 4
Ready in under 20 mins

1 medium onion, peeled and
    finely chopped

1 tbsp sunflower, vegetable or
    olive oil

24 mini beef meatballs (around
    400g)

½ tsp ground paprika

1 × 340g jar tomato pasta sauce
    (or home-made on page 204)

¼–½ tsp dried chilli flakes (optional)

This recipe uses ready-made meatballs and a jar of sauce to keep it super-speedy. You could also make it with 12 larger meatballs – just cut them in half before tossing with the paprika. You could also serve this piled into warmed rolls or wraps and topped with lots of grated cheese.

Mix the onion with the oil in a shallow microwaveable dish (the meatballs will need to be in a single layer when they cook, so make sure the dish has a wide base).

Toss the meatballs with the paprika in a bowl and scatter on top of the onion. Cover and cook on HIGH for 5 mins (1000W), 6 mins 10 secs (800W), or until the onion is softened and the meatballs are cooked.

Pour the sauce over the meatballs and onion, add the chilli, if using, and toss lightly. Cover and cook on HIGH for 5 mins (1000W) or 6 mins 10 secs (800W), stirring halfway.

Leave to stand for 5 mins before serving; this resting stage will make the meatballs more tender.

Add seasoning to taste and serve with pasta.

Micro-tip — You can
use lamb or pork meatballs, if you
prefer.

Super-quick Chilli

Serves 4–5
Ready in under 30 mins

400g extra-lean minced beef
(5% fat)
1 medium onion, peeled and finely
chopped
1 tsp each ground coriander, ground
cumin and hot smoked paprika
1 beef stock cube (preferably Oxo)
1 × 400g can mixed beans in chilli
sauce
1 × 400g can chopped tomatoes
2 tbsp tomato purée
1 tsp dried oregano

A rich, healthy chilli in less than 30 mins seems impossible – but it's not. A great midweek meal, serve this with rice, in tacos or spooned into jacket potatoes. Any leftovers will freeze brilliantly for up to 4 months.

Put the mince, onion, spices and crumbled stock cube in a large, wide-based microwaveable dish or casserole. Season with salt and ground black pepper. Using your hands, mix everything together really well, so the onion and spices are evenly dispersed through the mince.

Cover and cook on HIGH for 3 mins (1000W) or 3 mins 40 secs (800W). Break up the meat with two spatulas or spoons using a vertical chopping action (see tip on page 224). This takes a while but is worth the effort for a good end result, I promise!

Cover and cook on HIGH for 2 mins (1000W) or 2 mins 30 secs (800W). Break up the meat thoroughly once more.

Add the beans in sauce, tomatoes, tomato purée and oregano, season with salt and plenty of ground black pepper and stir well. Return to the microwave, cover and cook on HIGH for 10 mins (1000W) or 12 mins 30 secs (800W), stirring halfway.

Serve with rice and try it with sliced avocado, grated cheese, soured cream and freshly chopped coriander, if you like. I serve mine with pink pickled onions, too (page 212).

Micro-tips —— If you can't get hold of mixed beans in chilli sauce, use kidney beans in chilli sauce or similar.

If your mince is sold in 500g packets, use the whole amount to prevent waste – the cooking times won't change.

Simple Beef Stew and Dumplings

Serves 4
Ready in under 40 mins

1 tbsp sunflower or vegetable oil

1 medium onion, peeled and finely
    chopped

1 celery stick, trimmed and cut into
    roughly 1cm slices

150g button mushrooms, halved

2–3 carrots (around 200g), peeled
    and cut into roughly 1cm slices

1 tsp yeast extract (such as Marmite)

1 × 400g can chopped tomatoes

100ml hot beef stock (made with
    1 stock cube)

1 tsp caster sugar

½ tsp dried mixed herbs

350–400g lean beef steak, trimmed
    of fat, cut in half lengthways,
    then cut widthways into 1cm
    thin slices

1 tsp ground paprika

freshly chopped parsley, to serve
    (optional)

For the dumplings

150g self-raising flour, plus extra
    for dusting

75g shredded beef suet

Micro-tip —— You could use
a cheap cut of beef, as long as it is
lean. Remove all the fat and cut the
beef widthways into short, thin slices
to help it remain tender.

A beef stew and dumplings in just over half an hour? It's perfectly possible with the help of a microwave oven. Now, I'm not going to say that the beef will be quite as tender as it would be after a long, slow cook, but if you have to get dinner on the table in a hurry, this hearty supper is well worth a go. The key is to get the first five ingredients cooking while you prepare the rest.

Mix the oil, onion, celery, mushrooms, carrots and yeast extract in a large, wide-based microwaveable casserole. Cover and cook on HIGH for 8 mins (1000W), 10 mins (800W), or until softened, stirring halfway.

Stir well, then add the tomatoes, beef stock, sugar, mixed herbs and season with ground black pepper. Cover and cook on HIGH for 5 mins (1000W), 6 mins 10 secs (800W), or until hot and bubbling.

Meanwhile, make the dumplings. Put the flour, suet and a good pinch of salt in a medium bowl. Toss together well, then stir in enough cold water to form a soft, spongy dough (roughly 125ml). Using floured hands, roll into 8 rough balls.

Put the beef in a bowl and toss with the paprika, a little salt and lots of ground black pepper. Stir the beef into the vegetables, then place the dumplings on top. Cover and cook on HIGH for 6 mins (1000W), 7 mins 30 secs (800W), or until the dumplings are well risen, light and fluffy.

Stand for 5 mins before serving sprinkled with the chopped parsley, if you like.

Simple Bolognese Sauce

Serves 4
Ready in under 30 mins

400–500g minced beef
1 medium onion, peeled and finely
    chopped
2 garlic cloves, peeled and crushed
1 tsp dried oregano
1 beef stock cube (preferably Oxo)
200g mushrooms (any kind), sliced
1 × 400g can chopped tomatoes
3 tbsp tomato purée
1 tsp caster sugar
finely grated Parmesan, to serve
    (optional)
fresh basil leaves, to serve (optional)

Perfect for anyone new to cooking, this easy Bolognese sauce is a cinch to make in the microwave. I've perfected all the timings, so there is very little to go wrong. Serve with freshly cooked pasta or pile into jacket potatoes (page 34), roll into wraps or spoon onto toasted French bread for the ultimate sloppy Joe. What's more, the sauce will freeze brilliantly for at least 4 months and can be reheated from frozen in the microwave – what's not to like?

Put the mince, onion, garlic, oregano and crumbled stock cube in a large, wide-based microwaveable dish. Using your hands, mix everything together really well, so the onion is evenly dispersed through the mince.

Cover and cook on HIGH for 4 mins (1000W) or 5 mins (800W). Break up the meat with two spatulas or spoons using a vertical chopping action (see tip on page 224). This takes a while but is worth the effort for a good end result, I promise.

Cover and cook on HIGH for 2 mins (1000W) or 2 mins 30 secs (800W). Break up the meat thoroughly once more.

Add the mushrooms, tomatoes, tomato purée, sugar and 3 tablespoons water. Season with salt and plenty of ground black pepper. Stir well, cover and cook on HIGH for 10 mins (1000W) or 12 mins 30 secs (800W), stirring halfway.

Serve with pasta and top with finely grated Parmesan and fresh basil leaves, if you like.

Micro-tip —— If you have any red wine knocking around, use this instead of the water for an even richer flavour.

If your stock cube doesn't crumble easily, dissolve it in 3 tbsp just-boiled water and add with the mushrooms and tomatoes instead.

Massaman Beef Curry

Serves 4
Ready in under 35 mins

A massaman curry normally takes hours of simmering in the oven but my speedy version cooks in under 35 mins. You could choose a cheap cut of steak here, just make sure you cut it widthways into thin, short strips so it stays tender.

1 tbsp sunflower or vegetable oil

2 red onions, peeled and thinly sliced

500g potatoes (preferably Maris Piper), peeled and cut into roughly 2cm chunks

20g fresh root ginger, peeled and finely grated

2 garlic cloves, peeled and finely grated

2 tbsp red, green or massaman Thai curry paste (around 30g)

1 × 400g can coconut milk

2 tbsp dark soy sauce

1 tsp caster or soft brown sugar

½ beef stock cube (preferably Oxo)

300g lean beef steak, trimmed of fat and very thinly sliced widthways (see tip on page 224)

some freshly chopped coriander, peanuts, crispy fried onions and sliced chilli, to serve (optional)

Put the oil, onions and potatoes in a large, wide-based microwaveable bowl or casserole – it will need to be large enough to hold at least 2.5 litres liquid. Cover and cook on HIGH for 8 mins (1000W) or 10 mins (800W), stirring halfway.

Stir in the ginger, garlic and curry paste. Cover and cook on HIGH for 2 mins (1000W) or 2 mins 30 secs (800W).

Pour in the coconut milk, soy sauce and sugar, and crumble in the stock cube. Stir well. Cover and cook on HIGH for 7 mins (1000W), 8 mins 30 secs (800W), or until the potatoes are tender and the sauce is bubbling, stirring halfway. (Take care as the coconut milk will be very hot.)

Add the beef and stir well. Cover and cook on HIGH for 2 mins (1000W), 2 mins 30 secs (800W), or until the beef is almost cooked but with some pinkness remaining in the centre (it will continue cooking for a few secs after you remove it from the oven). Stir well.

Sprinkle with some chopped coriander, peanuts, crispy fried onions or chilli, if you like, and serve with rice.

Micro-tip —— For an even more authentic flavour, stir in a small handful of Makrut lime leaves at the same time as the coconut milk. A couple of tablespoons of peanut butter stirred in at the same time as the coconut milk will make the curry extra rich.

Rustic Shepherd's Pie

Serves 5
Ready in under 40 mins

1 tbsp sunflower or vegetable oil

1 medium onion, peeled and finely chopped

2–3 medium carrots (around 200g), peeled and cut into small chunks

1 celery stick, trimmed and cut into 5mm slices

400–500g lamb mince

1 tsp dried mixed herbs

3 tbsp tomato purée

2 tbsp Worcestershire sauce

300ml hot lamb stock (made with 1 cube)

2 tbsp cornflour mixed with 2 tbsp cold water

For the topping
4 large potatoes (preferably Maris Piper; each around 200g)

25g butter, diced

75g Cheddar, finely grated

pinch of dried parsley or 1 tsp Topping Mix (page 211) (optional)

A family-style shepherd's pie that can be cooked and served in the same dish. The potato topping is made from fluffy microwaved potatoes, so there is no need to mash them.

Prick the potatoes for the topping 4–5 times all over with a fork. Place on a microwaveable plate lined with microwave-safe kitchen paper (not recycled – see page 221). Cook on HIGH for 12 mins 40 secs (1000W), 16 mins (800W), or until soft, turning every 4–5 mins. Set aside.

Mix the oil, onion, carrots and celery in a large, wide-based microwaveable casserole or dish – it will need to be large enough to hold roughly 2.5 litres. Cover and cook on HIGH for 5 mins (1000W), 6 mins 10 secs (800W), or until the vegetables are soft.

Add the mince and herbs, season well with salt and ground black pepper and mix well. Cover and cook on HIGH for 5 mins (1000W) or 6 mins 10 secs (800W), breaking up the meat halfway with two spatulas or spoons using a vertical chopping action (see tip on page 224). At the end of the cooking time, break up the meat again in the same way.

Whisk the tomato purée and Worcestershire sauce into the hot stock until dissolved. Pour over the mince, add the cornflour mixture and stir well. Cover and cook on HIGH for 5 mins (1000W) or 6 mins 10 secs (800W). Stir again.

Roughly chop the potatoes and arrange on top of the mince. Scatter the butter, cheese and parsley or Topping Mix over the top, if using. Season with salt and ground black pepper and cook uncovered on HIGH for 3 mins (1000W), 3 mins 40 secs (800W), or until the potatoes are hot.

Micro-tip —— If the potatoes are large, you may need to turn again and continue cooking for a further 1–2 mins.

Lamb Tagine

Serves 4–5
Ready in under 40 mins

2 tbsp olive or sunflower oil

½ medium onion, peeled and finely chopped

1 tsp ground cumin

1 tsp ground coriander

2 tbsp harissa paste (preferably rose harissa)

2 tbsp plain flour

1 × 400g can chopped tomatoes

150ml hot lamb stock (made with 1 stock cube)

1 × 400g can chickpeas, drained

2 tbsp tomato purée

2 tbsp runny honey

15g bunch fresh coriander, finely chopped, plus extra leaves to serve

For the meatballs

½ medium onion, peeled and finely chopped

1 tsp dried mint

1 tbsp harissa paste

400g lamb mince

2 tbsp plain flour

If you like a richly flavoured tagine, you'll love this easy lamb version simmered in the microwave. I've made simple meatballs, instead of using chunks of lamb, as they stay wonderfully tender and don't need pre-frying.

To make the meatballs, put the onion, mint and harissa in a large microwaveable mixing bowl. Season with a little salt and lots of ground black pepper. Stir together.

Cover and cook on HIGH for 2 mins (1000W) or 2 mins 30 seconds (800W), then stir well.

Add the lamb mince and flour and, using a spoon then hands, mix everything together really well, so the onion is evenly dispersed through the mince. Roll into 20 small evenly sized balls and set aside.

To make the sauce, put the oil, onion, spices and harissa in a large, wide-based microwaveable dish or casserole, and stir well. Cover and cook on HIGH for 4 mins (1000W) or 5 mins (800W), stirring halfway.

Stir in the flour then add the tomatoes, stock, chickpeas, tomato purée honey and coriander. Add the meatballs and stir gently into the sauce. Cover and cook on HIGH for 12 mins (1000W) or 15 mins (800W), stirring very gently every 4–5 minutes, or until the meatballs are cooked through and the sauce is bubbling. Take care not to break up the meatballs as you stir.

Leave to stand for 5 mins before sprinkling with the remaining coriander and serving with couscous, rice or flat breads.

Greek-style Lamb with Feta

Serves 4–5
Ready in under 30 mins

400–500g lamb mince

1 medium onion, peeled and finely
    chopped

2 garlic cloves, peeled and crushed

1 tsp dried oregano

½ tsp dried mint

generous pinch of ground cinnamon

1 lamb stock cube (preferably Oxo)

2 medium courgettes (around 275g
    total weight), trimmed and cut
    into 5mm slices

2 tbsp plain flour

3 tbsp tomato purée

1 × 400g can chopped tomatoes

75ml red wine or extra stock

200g feta cheese

fresh mint, to serve (optional)

I love a good moussaka but making one in the microwave can be a bit of a faff. This easy lamb dish is the perfect alternative when you crave that herby spicy lamb combo. I serve mine with crumbled feta, Greek yoghurt and warmed flat bread for mopping up all the lovely sauce.

Put the mince, onion, garlic, oregano, mint, cinnamon and crumbled stock cube in a large, wide-based microwaveable dish or casserole. Season with salt and lots of ground black pepper. Using hands, mix everything together really well, so the onion is evenly dispersed through the mince.

Cover and cook on HIGH for 3 mins (1000W) or 3 mins 40 secs (800W). Break up the meat with two spatulas or wooden spoons using a vertical chopping action (see tip on page 224). This takes a while but is worth the effort for a good end result, I promise!

Stir in the courgettes, cover and cook on HIGH for 3 mins (1000W), 3 mins 40 secs (800W), or until the courgettes are just tender.

Stir in the flour, then add the tomato purée, canned tomatoes and red wine or stock. Stir well, cover and cook on HIGH for 12 mins (1000W) or 15 mins (800W), stirring halfway.

Top with the crumbled feta and a few fresh mint leaves, if you like, and serve with yoghurt and some warmed flat breads or rice alongside.

Micro-tip —— If you don't have a stock cube that crumbles easily, dissolve it in 75ml just-boiled water and add at the same time as the tomatoes.

Harissa Lamb Burgers

Serves 4
Ready in under 15 mins

1 medium onion, peeled and finely
    chopped
1 tsp dried oregano
½ tsp dried mint
2 tbsp harissa paste (preferably
    rose harissa)
1 tbsp yeast extract (such as
    Marmite)
500g lamb mince
2 tbsp plain flour

Burgers in the microwave? Yes! And they are delicious – if you don't believe me, give them a go! These ones are made with lamb mince, herbs and spices.

Put the onion, oregano, mint, harissa and yeast extract in a large microwaveable mixing bowl. Season with a little salt and lots of ground black pepper. Stir together.

Cover and cook on HIGH for 2 mins (1000W) or 2 mins 30 secs (800W). Stir well – the yeast extract should have melted into the onion. Set aside to cool a little.

Add the lamb mince and flour. Using your hands, mix everything together really well, so the onion is evenly dispersed through the mince.

Divide into four portions and roll into balls. Flatten the balls into burger shapes, roughly 1.5cm deep. Place the burgers spaced apart on two large microwaveable plates.

Microwave one plate at a time on HIGH for 3 mins 10 secs (1000W), 4 mins (800W), or until the burgers are hot and cooked through.

Remove the burgers from the plates and discard any cooking juices that have collected underneath.

Serve in warm, toasted buns with salad and sliced tomatoes, mint and soured cream or yoghurt.

Micro-tip —— For a delicious topping, mix yoghurt with a little mint sauce and a pinch of sugar.

Bacon, Spinach and Tomato Gnocchi

Serves 3–4
Ready in under 20 mins

3 rashers lean back bacon (ideally smoked), cut into roughly 1.5cm slices

4 sun-dried tomatoes in oil (around 40g total weight), drained and sliced

1 garlic clove, peeled and finely sliced

pinch of dried chilli flakes (optional)

2 tsp olive or sunflower oil

250ml just-boiled water from a kettle

500g fresh potato gnocchi

100ml double cream

100g young spinach leaves

A great and ever-so-easy one-pan supper for four! This is very versatile – swap the bacon for sliced mushrooms for a meat-free version, or leave it out altogether.

Put the bacon in a large microwaveable bowl or casserole dish. Toss with the tomato, garlic, chilli, if using, and the oil. Cover and cook on HIGH for 2 mins (1000W) or 2 mins 30 secs (800W).

Pour in the just-boiled water, add the gnocchi and stir lightly. Cover and cook on HIGH for 6 mins 30 secs (1000W), 8 mins (800W), or until the gnocchi is tender, stirring halfway.

Stir in the cream and season with ground black pepper. Place the spinach leaves on top without stirring, cover and cook on HIGH for 2 mins (1000W), 2 mins 30 secs (800W), or until the sauce is hot and the spinach softened.

Stir well, add an extra splash of hot water, if needed, and season with a little more ground black pepper, if you like. Serve in warm bowls.

Micro-tip —— If making without the bacon, add ½ vegetable stock cube to the water.

Sausage Casserole

Serves 4
Ready in under 30 mins,
plus standing

6–8 sausages

2 tbsp sunflower or vegetable oil

1 medium onion, peeled and thinly
sliced

2 garlic cloves, peeled and crushed

1 red pepper, deseeded and cut into
slices

1 yellow pepper, deseeded and cut
into slices

1 tsp hot smoked paprika,
depending on taste

1 tsp dried oregano

1 × 400g can chopped tomatoes

1 × 400g can butterbeans, drained

2 tbsp tomato purée

2 tbsp white or red wine vinegar

3 tbsp soft dark brown sugar

freshly chopped parsley, to serve
(optional)

Sausages cook surprisingly well in the microwave but they won't brown as they would in a pan or under the grill. My solution is to serve them in a rich, tangy tomato sauce where any lack of colour won't be noticed but their flavour and texture is sure to be a hit.

To prepare the sausages, prick each one 4–5 times with a cocktail stick, or twice with a fork, to stop the skins bursting as they cook. Place 3–4 on a large microwaveable plate, cover and cook on HIGH for 2 mins (1000W), 2 mins 30 secs (800W), or until cooked through. Set aside and repeat with the remaining sausages.

To make the sauce, place the oil, onion, garlic, peppers, paprika, herbs, a little salt and lots of ground black pepper in a large, wide-based microwaveable dish or casserole – it will need to be large enough to hold at least 2.5 litres liquid. Stir well, cover and cook on HIGH for 8 mins (1000W), 10 mins (800W), or until the vegetables are tender, stirring halfway.

Add the tomatoes, butterbeans, tomato purée, vinegar and sugar. Stir well then cover and cook on HIGH for 8 mins (1000W) or 10 mins (800W), stirring halfway.

Stir the sausages into the sauce. Cover and cook on HIGH for 3 mins (1000W), 3 mins 40 secs (800W), or until the sausages are hot.

Leave to stand for 5 mins before sprinkling with freshly chopped parsley. Serve with crusty bread, rice or jacket potatoes.

Micro-tips —— Use spicy
sausages or generously herbed
sausages for extra colour and
flavour, if you like.

Use any canned beans you like.

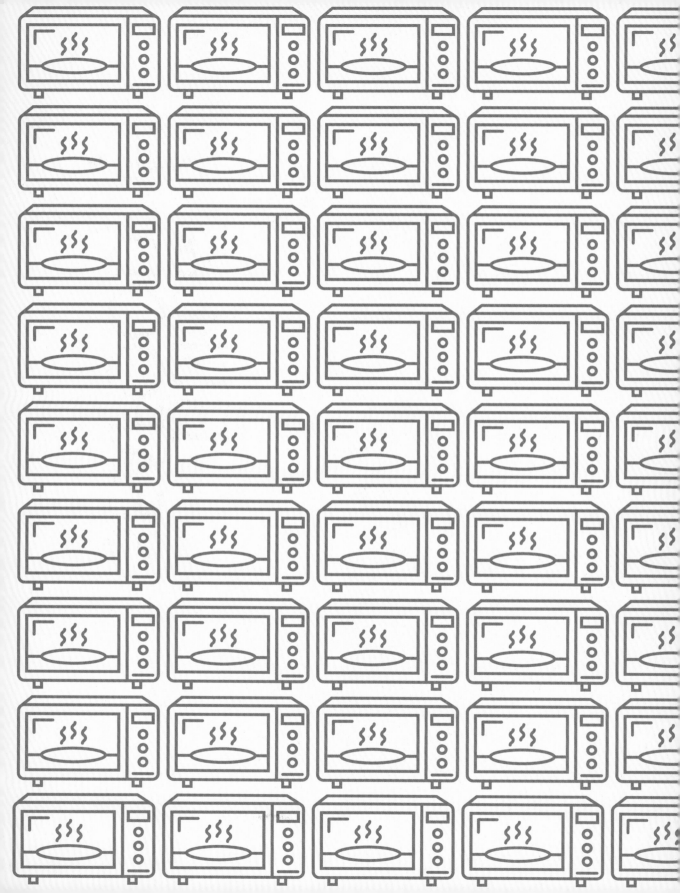

FISH & SEAFOOD

Cod with Cherry Tomatoes and Fresh Basil

Serves 2
Ready in under 10 mins

175g cherry tomatoes (around 16), halved
1 small garlic clove, peeled and finely grated or crushed
4 tbsp extra-virgin olive oil
2 thick fish fillets, such as cod or haddock (each around 140g)
fresh basil leaves, to serve

A lovely way to cook fish for a super-simple supper. Serve with crusty bread or new potatoes and alongside a salad or lightly cooked green vegetables.

Put the tomatoes into a wide-based, shallow microwaveable dish. Cover and cook on HIGH for 1 min (1000W) or 1 min 10 secs (800W).

Stir in the garlic, 2 tbsp of the oil, a good pinch of salt and a few twists of ground black pepper. Place the fish fillets on top of the tomatoes, skin-side down and a little way apart. Drizzle with the remaining oil and season with a little more pepper.

Cover the dish and cook on HIGH for 2 mins (1000W), 2 mins 30 secs (800W), or until just cooked – the exact timings will depend on the thickness of your fish.

Leave to stand for 5 mins without uncovering – the fish will continue cooking (see tip below). Top with fresh basil to serve.

Micro-tips —— If the fish isn't flaking easily when it's had its standing time, pop it back into the microwave and cook for a little longer.

Stir in a generous pinch of dried chilli flakes at the same time as the garlic, if you like a fiery flavour.

Mango and Cumin Salmon

Serves 2
Ready in under 10 mins

2 salmon fillets (each around 120g)
3 tsp mango chutney
¼ tsp cumin seeds
finely grated zest of ½ lime
lime wedges, to serve

For the salsa
½ ripe mango, peeled and diced
1 red chilli, finely sliced
juice of ½ lime
10g fresh coriander, leaves finely
    chopped

A super-quick and easy way to cook salmon. You can top the fillets with chilli jam instead of mango chutney, if you like. Serve as it is or with my fresh mango salsa.

Put the salmon, skin-side down, on a large microwaveable plate or shallow dish, with the thinner ends closest to the centre. Spread with the mango chutney and sprinkle with the cumin seeds and lime zest.

Cover with a microwave lid or an upturned microwaveable bowl and cook on HIGH for 1 min 30 secs (1000W), 1 min 50 secs (800W), or until the fish is almost fully cooked. Stop the microwave after 1 min and leave to stand for 1 min to allow the heat to redistribute before continuing (see tip on page 12).

Leave to stand for 5 mins without uncovering – the salmon will continue to cook.

Meanwhile, make the mango salsa by tossing all the ingredients together in a small bowl. Spoon over the salmon and serve with lime wedges.

Micro-tip —— The cooking time of the fish will depend on its shape, so if it isn't flaking when poked with a fork, pop it back into the microwave for a little longer.

Lime and Chilli Sea Bream with Coconut Rice

Serves 2
Ready in under 15 mins

2 sea bream or sea bass fillets
(each around 90g)
finely grated zest and juice of 1 lime,
plus wedges to serve
1 red chilli, finely sliced, or pinch of
dried chilli flakes
40g butter, diced
1 heaped tbsp finely chopped
coriander

For the coconut rice
1 small pepper (any colour),
deseeded and diced
50g frozen or canned sweetcorn
2 spring onions, trimmed and finely
sliced
1 × 250g pouch coconut rice

If you are ever stuck for ideas with fish, this easy recipe could be the answer. It only takes a few mins in the microwave, and cooks the fish perfectly, so you could have supper on the table in well under 15 mins.

To make the rice, put the pepper, sweetcorn and spring onions in a wide-based, shallow microwaveable dish. Cover and cook on HIGH for 1 min 30 secs (1000W) or 2 mins (800W).

Squeeze the coconut rice in the pouch to break it up, then snip the end and shake the rice into the dish with the vegetables. Stir well and season with lots of ground black pepper. Cover and cook on HIGH for 2 mins (1000W) or 2 mins 30 secs (800W).

Place the fish fillets, skin-side down, on the rice, spaced a little way apart. Drizzle over the lime juice and sprinkle with the lime zest and chilli. Season with a pinch of salt and ground black pepper.

Dot with the butter, sprinkle with the coriander, cover and cook on HIGH for 3 mins 10 secs (1000W), 4 mins (800W), or until the fish is just cooked – it should look white and flake into small pieces when prodded gently with a fork. If you don't have a turntable in your microwave, turn the dish halfway.

Leave to stand for 2–3 mins without uncovering.

Serve with lime wedges.

Micro-tip —— You can make this dish with other flavours of ready-made rice, or use freshly cooked.

Smoked Haddock Chowder

Serves 2
Ready in under 25 mins

A comforting smokey fish chowder that makes a welcoming lunch on a chilly day. I sometimes top mine with a poached egg for a simple supper – and I always serve it with crusty bread.

½ medium onion, peeled and finely chopped

1–2 large potatoes (around 300g), peeled and cut into roughly 1.5cm chunks

1 medium leek (around 175g), trimmed and thinly sliced

25g butter, cubed

15g plain flour

200ml milk

100ml just-boiled water from a kettle

200g skinless smoked haddock fillet, cut into roughly 2cm chunks

100g frozen or canned sweetcorn, thawed if frozen

2 heaped tbsp freshly chopped parsley, plus extra to serve (optional)

Put the onion and potatoes in a large, wide-based microwaveable dish or casserole. Cover and cook on HIGH for 4 mins (1000W), 5 mins (800W), or until the potato is softened, stirring halfway. (The potato will cook more quickly spread out in a dish with a flat bottom.)

Scatter the leek on top of the potato and onion and dot with the butter. Season with a little salt and lots of ground black pepper. Cover and cook on HIGH for 2 mins (1000W), 2 mins 30 secs (800W), or until the leek is just softened.

Stir the flour into the buttery vegetables, then slowly add the milk, followed by the just-boiled water, stirring all the time. Once all the liquid has been incorporated, cover and cook on HIGH for 4 mins (1000W) or 5 mins (800W), until thickened, stirring halfway.

Stir in the fish, sweetcorn and freshly chopped parsley. Cover and cook on HIGH for 2 mins 50 secs (1000W) or 3 mins 30 secs (800W).

Leave to stand for 5 mins.

Adjust the seasoning to taste and sprinkle with more parsley to serve, if you like.

Micro-tip —— This is delicious topped with a poached egg (page 25). You'll have time to cook the eggs while the chowder is standing.

Lemon Cod with Peas and Potatoes

Serves 2
Ready in under 15 mins

300g baby new potatoes, halved
100g frozen peas
40g butter, cubed
2 thick cod fillets or cod loin, with or
    without skin (each around 140g)
finely grated zest of ½ small lemon,
    plus wedges, to seve
freshly chopped dill, to serve
    (optional)

You can use any fish fillets for this simple, one pan supper. I use cod but haddock, salmon or thick trout fillets would also work well.

Put the potatoes in a single layer in a wide-based, shallow microwaveable dish and sprinkle with 1 tbsp cold water. Cover and cook on HIGH for 5 mins 20 secs (1000W), 6 mins 40 secs (800W), or until just tender, stirring halfway.

Add the peas and butter, taking care as there will be lots of steam when you lift the lid. Cover and cook on HIGH for 1 min (1000W), 1 min 10 secs (800W), or until hot.

Mix the buttery peas and potatoes together and top with the cod fillets.

Sprinkle the lemon zest over the cod and season with a little salt and lots of ground black pepper. Cover and cook on HIGH for 2 mins (1000W), 2 mins 30 secs (800W), or until the fish is just cooked. It should be firm and look opaque.

Leave to stand for 5 mins without uncovering – the fish will continue cooking.

Serve sprinkled with a little fresh dill, if you like, and with lemon wedges alongside.

Micro-tip —— The cooking time of the fish will depend on its shape, so if it isn't flaking in the middle when poked with a fork, pop it back into the microwave for a little longer.

Salmon with Leeks and Cream

Serves 2
Ready in under 15 mins

250g new potatoes, cut into roughly
    1cm slices
1 medium leek (around 175g),
    trimmed and cut into roughly
    1cm slices
25g butter, cubed
1 heaped tbsp freshly chopped
    parsley or chives, or ¼ tsp dried
    parsley or chives, plus extra, to
    serve (optional)
finely grated zest of ½ small lemon
2 salmon fillets (each around 120g)
6 tbsp double cream

An all-in-one dish that makes the perfect supper for two.
Serve with extra wedges of lemon, if you like.

Put the potatoes and leek in a shallow microwaveable dish, season with salt and ground black pepper and toss together lightly. Dot with the butter and sprinkle with the parsley or chives. Cover and cook on HIGH for 5 mins (1000W), 6 mins 10 secs (800W), or until the potatoes are tender, stirring halfway.

Sprinkle the vegetables with the lemon zest, then place the salmon fillets skin-side down on top.

Drizzle the cream mainly over the potatoes and leeks but a little over the salmon. Season with more ground black pepper, cover and cook on HIGH for 3 mins (1000W), 3 mins 40 secs (800W), or until the salmon is just cooked.

Leave to stand for 3–5 mins without uncovering – the fish will continue cooking.

Serve sprinkled with extra herbs, if you like.

Micro-tip —— If your salmon begins to 'pop', stop cooking and stand for 1 min to allow the heat to redistribute before continuing.

Simple Fish Stew

Serves 4
Ready in under 30 mins

4 tbsp extra-virgin olive oil

½ medium onion, peeled and finely chopped

2 garlic cloves, peeled and crushed

1 small–medium fennel bulb (around 200g), trimmed and very thinly sliced (save some of the fronds to garnish)

2 tsp ground coriander

1 x 500g carton passata

75ml white wine

small pinch of saffron

200ml hot vegetable or fish stock (made with 1 stock cube)

pinch of dried chilli flakes

1–2 bay leaves

400g thick skinless fish fillet, such as cod or haddock, cut into roughly 3cm chunks

150g cooked peeled prawns, thawed if frozen

freshly chopped parsley, to serve (optional)

An easy version of a classic French dish; I serve mine with a sprinkling of grated Gruyère, some garlic mayonnaise and toasted slices of French bread or ready-made crostini. You can use grated Parmesan or Cheddar instead of the Gruyère, if you like.

Put the oil, onion, garlic, fennel and coriander in a large, wide-based microwaveable dish or casserole and mix well. Cover and cook on HIGH for 8 mins (1000W), 10 mins (800W), or until the fennel is well softened, stirring halfway. Take care when you remove the lid as the vegetables will produce a lot of hot steam.

Add the passata, wine, saffron, stock, chilli flakes and bay leaves, and season with salt and ground black pepper. Cover and cook on HIGH for 6 mins (1000W) or 7 mins 30 secs (800W), stirring halfway.

Stir in the fish, cover and cook on HIGH for 2 mins (1000W) or 2 mins 30 secs (800W).

Stir lightly and take care not to break up the fish. Scatter the prawns on top, return to the microwave, cover and cook on HIGH for 2 mins (1000W), 2 mins 30 secs (800W), or until the prawns are hot and the fish is cooked through.

Leave to stand for 5 mins.

Scatter freshly chopped parsley or reserved fennel fronds to serve.

Micro-tips —— You can use any fish you like for this recipe.

A pouch or tub of ready-made fish stock is a great alternative to a cube.

Salmon with Ginger and Soy

Serves 4
Ready in under 20 mins

2 balls stem ginger (from a jar), cut into tiny matchsticks

2 tbsp dark soy sauce

3 tbsp runny honey

¼ tsp dried chilli flakes

1 garlic clove, peeled and finely sliced

4 salmon fillets (each around 120g)

3 spring onions, trimmed and finely sliced

1 red chilli, finely sliced (optional)

This is one of my favourite ways to cook salmon. I keep a jar of stem ginger in the fridge at all times. Adding tiny matchsticks of ginger to soy sauce and honey makes a brilliant glaze. The salmon can be eaten hot with fresh veg and microwave noodles, or cooled and added to a salad – great for a prep-ahead lunch.

Put the ginger, soy sauce, honey, chilli flakes and garlic in a wide-based, shallow microwaveable dish and mix well.

Add the salmon and turn a couple of times to coat in the glaze. The salmon should end up in single layer, skin-side down, spaced slightly apart, with the thinner ends closer to the centre (see tip on page 11).

Scatter with the spring onions and sliced chilli, if using, and season with a few twists of ground black pepper.

Cover and cook on HIGH for 4 mins (1000W), 5 mins (800W), or until the fish is almost fully cooked. Stop the microwave halfway through the cooking time and leave to stand for 2 mins to allow the heat to redistribute before continuing. (Also see tip on page 12.) If cooking in a microwave oven without a turntable, turn the dish at this point.

Leave to stand for 5 mins without uncovering – it will continue cooking.

Serve the salmon with the sauce drizzled over the top.

Micro-tip —— If you don't have stem ginger, add a little grated fresh root ginger or leave it out altogether – it will still be delicious!

Prawn Masala Curry

Serves 2–3
Ready in under 15 mins

2 tbsp sunflower or vegetable oil

½ medium onion, peeled and finely sliced

1 tbsp medium Indian-style curry paste (from a jar)

3 large ripe vine tomatoes (around 250g), roughly chopped

2 tbsp mango chutney

250–300g cooked peeled prawns, thawed if frozen

fresh coriander leaves, to serve

An almost effortless – and very delicious – prawn curry that uses ready-made curry paste for ease and mango chutney for sweetness. Serve with fluffy basmati rice or naan bread. If you don't fancy prawns, you can add chunks of fresh fish fillet instead. It makes two to three generous portions, or four if serving with other curries.

Put the oil and onion in a large microwaveable dish. Cover and cook on HIGH for 3 mins 10 secs (1000W), 4 mins (800W), or until softened, stirring halfway.

Stir in the curry paste, tomatoes and mango chutney. Cover and cook on HIGH for 4 mins (1000W), 5 mins (800W), or until the tomatoes break down and become soft and juicy, stirring halfway.

Stir in the prawns, cover and cook on HIGH for 1 min 30 secs (1000W), 1 min 50 secs (800W), or until hot.

Scatter the coriander over to serve.

Micro-tip —— If you want to use raw prawns, cook for 1–2 mins longer, stirring halfway, until hot and pink throughout.

Garlic and Chilli Prawns

Serves 2–3
Ready in under 10 mins

4–6 garlic cloves, depending on size,
    peeled and very thinly sliced
2 plump red chillies, finely chopped,
    or ½ tsp dried chilli flakes
100ml light olive oil
200g peeled raw king prawns,
    thawed if frozen
2–3 tbsp freshly chopped parsley
    (optional)

A brilliantly simple starter or light supper. You can use any frozen prawns for this dish, but plump king prawns suit it particularly well. If you use cooked prawns instead of the raw ones, you can reduce the cooking time slightly.

Put the garlic, chilli and oil in a shallow microwaveable bowl. Cover and cook on HIGH for 1 min 30 secs (1000W) or 2 mins (800W), stirring halfway. The oil should be just warmed and the garlic and chilli softened; don't allow to overheat.

Add the prawns, season with a little salt and ground black pepper and toss lightly in the oil. Cover and cook on HIGH for 1 min (1000W), 1 min 10 secs (800W), stirring after 30 secs, or until completely pink through.

Stir in the chopped parsley, if using, and season with a little more black pepper.

Serve hot with warm crusty bread.

Micro-tip —— If you don't have any light olive oil, use half extra-virgin olive oil and half sunflower or vegetable oil instead.

Family Fish Pie

Serves 4–5
Ready in under 30 mins

350ml milk

480g mixed skinless fish, including
    smoked haddock, white fish,
    such as cod, and salmon, cut into
    roughly 3cm chunks

25g butter, cubed

25g plain flour

2 heaped tbsp finely chopped fresh
    parsley or dill

finely grated zest of ½ small lemon

4 tbsp double cream

50g baby spinach leaves

For the topping
650g Easiest Mashed Potatoes
    (page 210) or frozen mashed
    potatoes

4 tbsp double cream

1 tsp Crunchy Topping Mix
    (page 211)(optional)

Making fish pie from scratch in the microwave saves a whole lot of bother, especially if you use frozen mashed potatoes jazzed up with a splash of cream. The key to making it quickly is to cook the mash while you are preparing the other ingredients.

To make the topping, either follow the recipe on page 210 or scatter the frozen mashed potatoes into a wide-based microwaveable dish. Cover and cook on HIGH for 8 mins (1000W), 10 mins (800W), or until hot, stirring halfway.

Beat the cream into the mash and set aside.

Put the milk in a large microwaveable dish. Add the fish and stir lightly. Cover and cook on HIGH for 4 mins (1000W) or 5 mins (800W).

Drain the fish in a colander over a large microwaveable bowl, reserving the milk. Once drained, scatter the fish into a 1.5-litre, shallow microwaveable pie dish.

Whisk the butter, flour, parsley or dill, lemon zest and double cream into the warm milk. Cover and cook on HIGH for 2 mins (1000W), 2 mins 30 secs (800W), or until beginning to thicken, whisking halfway.

Whisk the sauce again, then season to taste with salt and ground black pepper and stir in the spinach. Cover and cook on HIGH for 2 mins (1000W), 2 mins 30 secs (800W), or until the spinach wilts and the sauce is thick.

Pour the sauce over the fish and stir gently. Spoon the mashed potato gently on top of the fish and spread evenly. Sprinkle with the Topping Mix, if using, and season with ground black pepper. Cook uncovered on HIGH for 4 mins (1000W), 5 mins (800W), or until the potato is hot. (Turn the dish halfway through the cooking time, if your microwave doesn't have a turntable.)

Micro-tip —— Use any fish you like, or buy ready-mixed packs, if you prefer. You can also swap some of the fish for prawns.

MEAT-FREE

Tomato Orzo Risotto

Serves 2–3
Ready in under 20 mins

1 × 400g can chopped tomatoes

2 garlic cloves, peeled and finely grated

2 tbsp extra-virgin olive oil

½ tsp dried oregano

150g dried orzo pasta

250ml hot vegetable stock (made with ½ stock cube)

40g Parmesan, finely grated, plus extra to serve

A quick one-pot supper that's made with mainly store cupboard ingredients. If you don't have Parmesan to hand, you can use any other cheese.

Put the tomatoes, garlic, oil, oregano and orzo in a large, deep microwaveable bowl or casserole.

Add a good pinch of salt and a few twists of ground black pepper. Stir in the stock. The pasta should be completely submerged in liquid. Cover and cook on HIGH for 10–12 mins, or until the orzo is tender, stirring halfway. (The cooking time doesn't vary much between wattages.)

Stir in the Parmesan, cover and leave to stand for 2–3 mins before serving with more cheese.

Creamy Pasta with Peas and Lemon

Serves 2
Ready in under 20 mins

175g dried penne pasta

500ml just-boiled water from a
    kettle

1 tbsp olive or sunflower oil

100g full-fat soft cheese (such as
    Philadelphia)

finely grated zest of ½ lemon

100g frozen peas

Parmesan or lemon zest, finely
    grated, to serve (optional)

Pasta in the microwave? Yup, it's perfectly possible. And while I don't think there is much point if you are cooking for more than two as the time saving isn't huge – this is actually a brilliant way to prepare a simple supper if you aren't a confident cook.

Put the penne in a very large, deep microwaveable bowl – it will need to hold at least 3 litres of liquid, as the water needs to boil freely for this recipe. Put the bowl on a microwaveable plate, then stir in the just-boiled water and oil. Cover and cook on HIGH for about 11 mins, or until tender, stirring after 6 mins. (The cooking time doesn't vary much between wattages.)

Carefully drain the pasta over a large bowl to catch the water and return the pasta to the dish. Add 5 tbsp of the hot pasta cooking water to the dish, then stir in the soft cheese and mix well.

Stir in the lemon zest and season with ground black pepper. Add a splash more water, if needed, so the sauce is light and creamy.

Meanwhile, cook the peas in a microwaveable bowl on HIGH for 1 min (1000W), 1 min 10 secs (800W), or until thawed.

Add the peas to the pasta and toss everything together. Cook on HIGH for 2 mins (1000W), 2 mins 30 secs (800W), or until hot.

Season to taste with salt and ground black pepper, and sprinkle with grated Parmesan or lemon zest to serve, if you like.

Micro-tip —— Placing your bowl on a microwaveable plate will make it easier to remove from the microwave. The water will be very hot, so take care.

Spanish-style Vegetable Pilaf

Serves 4
Ready in under 25 mins

2 tbsp extra-virgin olive oil

1 medium onion, peeled and finely
chopped

2 garlic cloves, peeled and thinly
sliced

200g basmati rice

1 tsp hot smoked paprika

good pinch of saffron strands

500ml hot vegetable stock (made
with 1 stock cube)

175g char-grilled artichokes from
a jar, drained and sliced or
quartered

175g roasted peppers from a jar,
drained and sliced

85g pitted black olives (preferably
Kalamata)

freshly chopped parsley and lemon
wedges, to serve (optional)

This colourful dish has all the flavour of a really good vegetarian paella and cooks perfectly in the microwave – great if you worry about getting rice right. Serve just as it is, or add a little crumbled goat's cheese at the end.

Put the oil, onion and garlic in a large, deep, wide-based, lidded microwaveable dish or casserole – it will need to be large enough to hold at least 2.5 litres. Cover and cook on HIGH for 4 mins (1000W) or 5 mins (800W), stirring halfway.

Stir in the rice, paprika and saffron and season well with salt and ground black pepper.

Pour in the stock and stir – the rice should be fully submerged in liquid.

Scatter the artichokes, peppers and olives on top without stirring. Cover and cook on HIGH for 10 mins (1000W), 12 mins (800W), or until the rice is tender and the liquid has been absorbed.

Leave to stand without uncovering for 5 mins.

Fluff with a fork, sprinkle with fresh parsley and serve with lemon wedges, if you like.

Micro-tip —— A good pinch of saffron is around ½ heaped tsp loosely packed. Swap the artichokes for sun-blush (semi-dried) tomatoes, if you like, or use a mixture.

Mushroom Pilau

Serves 4–6
Ready in under 25 mins

Fool-proof fluffy rice mildly spiced and tossed with juicy sultanas and toasted almonds. Serve as a main meal for four with chapatis, mango chutney, lime pickle and yoghurt, or as a side dish for six.

1 tsp cumin seeds

2 tbsp sunflower or vegetable oil

1 medium onion, peeled and finely chopped

200g mushrooms (any kind), sliced or quartered if small

2 garlic cloves, peeled and very thinly sliced

1 tbsp garam masala or curry powder

200g basmati rice

450ml just-boiled water from a kettle

50g sultanas or raisins

50g toasted flaked almonds

50g butter, diced

fresh coriander and melted butter, to serve (optional)

Put the cumin seeds and 1 tbsp of the oil in a large, deep, wide-based microwaveable dish or casserole – it will need to be large enough to hold at least 2.5 litres. Cover and cook on HIGH for 1 min 30 secs (1000W) or 2 mins (800W).

Add the onion, mushrooms, garlic, garam masala or curry powder and the remaining oil, season well with salt and lots of ground black pepper and toss together. Cover and cook on HIGH for 5 mins (1000W), 6 mins 10 secs (800W), or until softened, stirring halfway.

Add the rice and just-boiled water to the dish and stir well. Cover and cook on HIGH for 9 mins (1000W), 11 mins 10 secs (800W), or until the rice is tender and the liquid has been absorbed.

Stir in the sultanas or raisins, almonds and butter. Cover and leave to stand for 5 mins.

Serve with fresh coriander and a little melted butter drizzled on top, if you like.

Micro-tip —— Serve the rice topped with quartered hard-boiled eggs for a simple biryani-style dish.

Sweet Potato and Lentil Curry

Serves 4
Ready in under 25 mins

2 tbsp sunflower or vegetable oil

1 medium onion, peeled and finely chopped

3 medium sweet potatoes (around 500g total weight), peeled and cut into roughly 1.5cm chunks

2 tbsp medium Indian curry paste from a jar

1 × 400g can lentils (any kind), drained

1 × 400g can coconut milk

100g young spinach leaves

yoghurt and freshly chopped coriander, to serve (optional)

A warming meat-free curry that is delicious served with rice or warmed naan bread. It's great as a wintery lunch or supper, served with plenty of natural yoghurt and chutney. You'll find jars of Indian-style curry pastes in the world food section of the supermarket, but you could use 2–3 tbsp curry powder instead.

Put the oil, onion and sweet potatoes in a large, wide-based microwaveable dish or casserole and toss together well – it will need to be large enough to hold around 2.5 litres. Cover and cook on HIGH for 8 mins (1000W), 10 mins (800W), or until the sweet potato is tender, stirring halfway.

Stir in the curry paste, cover and cook on HIGH for 1 min (1000W) or 1 min 10 secs (800W).

Stir in the lentils and coconut milk and place the spinach leaves on top. Cover and cook on HIGH for 5 mins (1000W), 6 mins 10 secs (800W), or until gently simmering, rich and creamy, stirring the spinach into the curry halfway. Season with a little salt.

Scatter with fresh coriander and serve with yoghurt, if you like.

Micro-tip —— Make sure the sweet potato chunks are small so they cook more quickly. The larger they are, the longer they will take.

Rich Mushroom Casserole

Serves 4
Ready in under 30 mins

10g dried mushrooms, any kind,
    broken into small pieces
1 vegetable stock cube
2 tbsp tomato purée
1 tsp dried mixed herbs
300ml just-boiled water from
    a kettle
1 medium onion, peeled and finely
    chopped
2 tbsp sunflower or vegetable oil
300g small mushrooms (ideally
    chestnut), halved
2 garlic cloves, peeled and finely
    sliced
1 tbsp plain flour
50ml red wine or water
180g cooked chestnuts from
    a pouch or jar, halved
freshly chopped parsley, to serve
    (optional)

A luxurious-tasting vegetarian casserole that makes a great midweek meal and is special enough to serve for friends. It is possible to make it without the dried mushrooms but their rich mushroom-y flavour makes this dish particularly delicious.

Put the dried mushrooms, crumbled stock cube, tomato purée and herbs in a measuring jug and cover with the just-boiled water. Stir and leave to stand while the other ingredients are prepared.

Mix the onion and oil in a large, wide-based microwaveable dish or casserole. Cover and cook on HIGH for 4 mins (1000W) or 5 mins (800W), stirring halfway.

Stir the fresh mushrooms and garlic into the casserole. Season with a little salt and lots of ground black pepper. Cover and cook on HIGH for 4 mins (1000W) or 5 mins (800W).

Stir in the flour until thoroughly mixed with the vegetables, then pour in the dried mushrooms and their soaking liquor, the wine or water and add the chestnuts. Cover and cook on HIGH for 12 mins (1000W), 15 mins (800W), or until the sauce is rich and glossy and the mushrooms are tender, stirring halfway.

Scatter with fresh parsley to serve, if you like.

Micro-tip —— If you don't have any chestnuts, you can use canned or jarred butterbeans instead.

Vegetable Tagine

Serves 4
Ready in under 25 mins

A lightly spiced vegetable stew that goes brilliantly with couscous, flat bread or rice. Serve it with generous spoonfuls of Greek-style yoghurt, if you like. It will keep well in the fridge for up to 3 days.

2 tbsp extra-virgin olive, sunflower or vegetable oil
1 medium red onion, peeled and finely chopped
½ medium butternut squash (around 500g), peeled and cut into roughly 2cm chunks
1 medium courgette, trimmed, halved lengthways and cut into roughly 1.5cm slices
1 pepper (any colour), deseeded and cut into roughly 2cm chunks
2 garlic cloves, peeled and very thinly sliced
2 tsp ground coriander
2 tbsp harissa paste
1 × 400g can chopped tomatoes
1 × 400g can chickpeas, drained
100g dried apricots, quartered
2 tbsp tomato purée
3 tbsp runny honey
freshly chopped parsley, thyme or coriander, to serve (optional)

Mix the oil, onion and squash in a large, wide-based microwaveable bowl or casserole. Cover and cook on HIGH for 4 mins (1000W) or 5 mins (800W).

Add the courgette and pepper, cover and cook on HIGH for 4 mins (1000W) or 5 mins (800W), stirring halfway.

Season with salt and ground black pepper, then stir in the garlic, coriander and harissa paste. Microwave uncovered on HIGH for 1 min (1000W) or 1 min 10 secs (800W).

Stir in all the remaining ingredients, except the fresh herbs, plus 150ml water. Cover and cook on HIGH for 8 mins (1000W), 10 mins (800W), or until the vegetables are tender and the sauce is hot, stirring halfway.

Scatter with fresh herbs to serve, if you like.

Micro-tip —— Choose good-quality canned tomatoes for the best flavour, or add 3 tbsp tomato purée and ½ tsp sugar, if using an economy brand.

Quick Ratatouille

Serves 4
Ready in under 25 mins

3 tbsp extra-virgin olive oil, plus extra
    for drizzling
1 medium red onion, peeled and
    thinly sliced
1 large courgette (around 200g),
    trimmed, halved lengthways and
    cut into roughly 2cm slices
1 medium aubergine (around 200g),
    cut into roughly 2cm chunks
1 large red or yellow pepper,
    deseeded and cut into roughly
    2cm chunks
4 garlic cloves, peeled and very
    thinly sliced
1 tsp dried oregano
1 × 400g can chopped tomatoes
2 tbsp tomato purée
1 tsp caster sugar
fresh basil leaves, to serve (optional)

A perfectly cooked ratatouille is so easy in the microwave. You can serve this just as it is with crusty bread, or as an accompaniment to grilled or roasted meats and fish. It's also great tossed with pasta and served topped with loads of grated cheese.

Put the oil and onion in a large, wide-based microwaveable dish or casserole. Cover and cook on HIGH for 4 mins (1000W) or 5 mins (800W).

Add the courgette, aubergine, pepper and garlic, sprinkle over the oregano and season with salt and ground black pepper. Toss everything together. Cover and cook on HIGH for 8 mins (1000W), 10 mins (800W), or until the vegetables are tender, stirring halfway.

Stir in the tomatoes, tomato purée and sugar. Cover and cook on HIGH for 4 mins (1000W), 5 mins (800W), or until the sauce is hot.

Leave to stand for 5 mins without uncovering, then stir, adjust the seasoning to taste and scatter with fresh basil leaves, if using.

Serve warm or cold topped with a drizzle of oil and lots of crusty bread.

Micro-tip —— To make this into a heartier meal, stir in one or two cans of drained beans at the same time as the tomatoes. You will have to adjust the cooking time.

Vegetable Lasagne

Serves 4–5
Ready in under 40 mins

2 tbsp olive, sunflower or
    vegetable oil
1 large courgette (around 200g),
    trimmed, quartered lengthways
    and cut into roughly 2cm slices
2 large peppers (any colour),
    deseeded and cut into roughly
    2cm chunks
150g small chestnut mushrooms,
    sliced
1 tbsp plain flour
500g ready-made tomato pasta
    sauce from a jar (or home-made
    page 204)
180g fresh lasagne sheets
    (roughly 6)
2 tsp Crunchy Topping Mix (page
    211) (optional)

For the cheese sauce
30g butter, cubed
30g plain flour
300ml milk
100g mature Cheddar, finely grated

This lasagne is very adaptable – feel free to add any vegetables you like. I use fresh lasagne to cut back on the cooking time but you could use dried lasagne sheets if you pre-cook them first.

Mix the oil, courgette, peppers and mushrooms in a large, deep, wide-based microwaveable bowl or casserole. Season with lots of ground black pepper. Cover and cook on HIGH for 10 mins (1000W), 12 mins (800W), or until softened, stirring halfway.

Drain the vegetables in a colander, reserving any liquid, then return the vegetables to the dish. Add the flour, then slowly pour the reserved liquid back in, stirring all the time.

Stir the tomato sauce into the vegetables and set aside.

To make the cheese sauce, put the butter in a large microwaveable bowl. Cook uncovered on HIGH for 20 secs (1000W), 30 secs (800W), or until melted. Stir in the flour, then whisk in the milk. Add a good pinch of salt and a little ground black pepper. Cover and cook on HIGH for 4 mins (1000W), 5 mins (800W), or until the sauce is smooth and thick, whisking halfway. Stir in half the cheese and adjust the seasoning to taste.

Spoon roughly a third of the vegetable mixture into a shallow microwaveable dish (roughly 20cm square) – it will need to hold around 1.5 litres. Cover with lasagne sheets in a single layer – cut to fit, if necessary – then repeat the layers twice more until all the vegetable sauce is used and finish with a layer of pasta on top.

Pour the cheese sauce over, then sprinkle with the remaining cheese and the Topping Mix, if using. Cook uncovered on HIGH for 14 mins (1000W), 17 mins 30 secs (800W), or until the cheese has melted, the lasagne sheets are soft and the sauce is hot throughout. The exact cooking time will depend on the shape of your dish.

Leave to stand for 5 mins before serving.

Micro-tip
—— If you don't have a turntable, turn the lasagne to face the opposite direction every 5 mins through the cooking time.

Loaded Sweet Potatoes

Serves 2
Ready in under 15 mins

2 sweet potatoes (each around
    250g), well washed
1 red or yellow pepper, deseeded
    and diced
1 × 400g can beans in chilli sauce
½ x 195g can sweetcorn, drained, or
    70g frozen sweetcorn
40g mature Cheddar, finely grated
soured cream, to serve (optional)

Cans of beans in chilli sauce make a perfect quick filling for sweet potatoes. Feel free to swap the beans for another favourite topping – leftover curry, chilli or Bolognese would all work well.

Prick each potato 4–5 times with a fork and place them spaced a little way apart on a microwaveable plate lined with a sheet of plain, microwave-safe kitchen paper (not recycled – see page 221). Cook on HIGH for 7 mins (1000W), 8 mins 40 secs (800W), or until tender, turning over halfway through. Set aside while the filling is prepared.

Put the pepper in a large microwaveable bowl and cook uncovered on HIGH for 2 mins (1000W), 2 mins 30 secs (800W), or until soft.

Add the beans and sweetcorn to the pepper and stir well.

Place each potato on a separate microwaveable plate. Make a cross in the centre of each one and open out.

Divide the vegetable mixture between the potatoes and top with the cheese. Cook one at a time uncovered on HIGH for 1 min 30 secs (1000W), 2 mins (800W), or until the cheese melts and the filling is hot.

Top with soured cream, if using, and serve.

Micro-tip —— The exact timings will vary according to the shape and weight of your potatoes, but you can test them by inserting a skewer or the tip of a small knife into the middle. It should slide in easily. If the potatoes remain a little hard, cook for longer, testing again every 30 secs.

Cheat's Macaroni Cheese

Serves 2
Ready in under 15 mins

It might seem strange to cook pasta in the microwave but it's actually a very easy way to prepare a one-pot meal – great if you aren't a confident cook.

150g dried macaroni or penne pasta
500ml just-boiled water from a
    kettle
1 tbsp sunflower or vegetable oil
150g full-fat soft cheese (such as
    Philadelphia)
75g mature Cheddar, finely grated
2 tsp Crunchy Topping Mix (page
    211) or a pinch of ground paprika
    (optional)

Put the pasta in a large, deep microwaveable bowl – it will need to hold at least 3 litres. Place the dish or bowl on a plate, stir in the just-boiled water and oil, cover and cook on HIGH for 10 mins (1000W), 11 mins (800W), or until tender, stirring after 5 mins. Take care as the steam will be hot when you remove the lid or film.

Drain the pasta in a colander, reserving the cooking liquid, then return the pasta to the bowl.

Add 5 tbsp of the pasta water, the soft cheese and roughly two thirds of the Cheddar to the pasta. Mix until the cheese melts and forms a creamy sauce.

Season with ground black pepper and sprinkle with the remaining Cheddar and Topping Mix or paprika, if using. Cook uncovered on HIGH for 2 mins (1000W), 2 mins 30 secs (800W), or until hot throughout.

Micro-tip —— You can divide the creamy pasta between two microwaveable bowls before sprinkling with the remaining Cheddar, if you like. You could add extra ingredients at this point, too, such as halved cherry tomatoes or strips of smoked salmon. Cook the bowls one at a time until hot throughout.

Spiced Cauliflower with Almonds

Serves 2–3
Ready in under 10 mins

1 small cauliflower (around 600g),
    trimmed and cut into small
    florets
2 tbsp olive, sunflower or
    vegetable oil
½ tsp cumin seeds
1 tbsp ground coriander
2 tsp garam masala or medium curry
    powder
1 tsp ground turmeric
100g full-fat Greek-style yoghurt
a drizzle of pomegranate molasses
80g pomegranate seeds
25g toasted flaked almonds
fresh coriander, to serve

Served warm or cold, this lightly spiced cauliflower is a great addition to any salad or can be eaten as an accompaniment to grilled meats or fish.

Cut the florets in half or quarters, if they are large – they need to be roughly the same size to cook evenly.

Put the cauliflower into a shallow microwaveable dish and toss with the oil and spices.

Season generously with salt and lots of ground black pepper and toss well together. Cover and cook on HIGH for 8 mins (1000W) or 10 mins (800W), stirring halfway. The cauliflower should be tender and the spices mellow; if not, pop back in the microwave for a further 1–2 mins.

Drizzle with the yoghurt and pomegranate molasses, and sprinkle with pomegranate seeds, almonds and fresh coriander, if using, to serve.

Spiced Potatoes and Peas

Serves 2–4
Ready in under 25 mins

600g medium potatoes (preferably
 Maris Piper), peeled and cut into
 roughly 2cm chunks
1 medium onion, peeled and finely
 chopped
2 tbsp sunflower or vegetable oil
3 garlic cloves, peeled and very
 finely sliced
10g fresh root ginger, peeled and
 finely chopped
½ tsp fine sea salt
1 tsp cumin seeds
1 tsp garam masala
1 tsp ground turmeric
125g frozen peas
naan bread and mango chutney,
 to serve (optional)

You could serve these lightly spiced potatoes on their own as a light meal for two, as an accompaniment, or sandwiched in warm naan bread spread with mango chutney.

Mix the potatoes and onion in a large, wide-based microwaveable dish or casserole. Stir in the oil, cover and cook on HIGH for 8 mins (1000W), or 10 mins (800W), stirring halfway.

Sprinkle the potatoes and onion with the garlic, ginger, salt, cumin seeds, garam masala and ground turmeric. Season with lots of ground black pepper and toss together well. Cover and cook on HIGH for 4 mins (1000W), 5 mins (800W) or until the potatoes are soft.

Stir in the peas, cover and cook on HIGH for 2 mins (1000W), 2 mins 30 secs (800W), or until hot.

Check the seasoning and serve with warmed naan bread and mango chutney, if you like.

Speedy Cauliflower Cheese

Serves 2–4
Ready in under 20 mins

1 medium cauliflower (around 800g), trimmed and broken into florets
40g butter, cubed
40g plain flour
400ml milk
80g mature Cheddar, finely grated
2 tsp Crunchy Topping Mix (page 211) (optional)

You can serve this as an accompaniment for four or a light meal for two. Cooking it in the microwave will free up space on the hob and oven. I like to serve it as a simple lunch with hunks of warm, buttered bread.

Cut the florets in half or quarters, if they are large – they need to be roughly the same size to cook evenly.

Put the cauliflower in a shallow microwaveable dish. They shouldn't be packed too tightly. Sprinkle over 3 tbsp cold water, cover and cook on HIGH for 8 mins (1000W), 10 mins (800W), or until just tender, stirring halfway. (The timings will depend on the size and shape of your dish and the size of the florets.)

Put the butter in a large microwaveable bowl, cover and cook on HIGH for 30 secs (1000W), 40 secs (800W), or until melted.

Stir the flour into the melted butter, then whisk in the milk. Add a good pinch of salt and a little ground black pepper. Cover and cook on HIGH for 5 mins (1000W) or 6 mins (800W), whisking well after 3 mins, then whisking every minute until the sauce is smooth and thick.

Stir in roughly three-quarters of the cheese, then add a little more salt or ground black pepper, if needed.

Pour the cheese sauce over the cooked cauliflower. Sprinkle with the remaining cheese, then the Topping Mix, if using. Season with more ground black pepper and cook on HIGH for 2 mins (1000W), 2 mins 30 secs (800W), or until the cheese topping melts and the cauliflower is hot.

Micro-tip —— Add 1 tsp mustard to the sauce at the same time as the cheese for an extra tangy flavour.

DESSERTS

Sticky Toffee Pudding

Serves 6–8
Ready in under 20 mins

sunflower or vegetable oil, for
    greasing
150g stoned soft dates, chopped
    small
100g butter, cubed
2 large eggs
100g soft dark brown sugar
150g self-raising flour
1 tsp bicarbonate of soda

For the sauce
75g butter, cubed
75g soft dark brown sugar
50g pecan nuts, roughly chopped
150ml double cream

A gorgeous, ever-popular dessert that's actually better cooked in the microwave and can be ready to serve in under 20 mins. Delicious served warm with vanilla ice cream.

Lightly oil a shallow microwaveable dish – it will need to be large enough to hold roughly 1.5 litres.

Put the dates in a medium microwaveable bowl and stir in 100ml water. Cook uncovered on HIGH for 1 min 30 secs (1000W) or 2 mins (800W), then leave to stand for around 5 mins to soften.

Put the butter in a large microwaveable mixing bowl, cover and cook on HIGH for 40 secs (1000W), 50 secs (800W), or until melted.

Add the eggs, sugar and flour to the bowl with the butter and beat with a wooden spoon until smooth and creamy.

Stir the bicarbonate of soda into the dates until they look frothy, then stir both into the cake batter.

Pour into the prepared dish and cook on HIGH for about 4 mins 30 secs (1000W), 5 mins 40 secs (800W), or until well risen and firm. A skewer inserted into the centre of the cake should come out clean. The exact timing will depend on the shape of your dish. Leave to stand while the sauce is made.

To make the sauce, put the butter, sugar, nuts and cream in a medium microwaveable bowl and cook uncovered on HIGH for 2 mins (1000W), 2 mins 30 secs (800W), or until the sauce is thick and glossy, stirring halfway.

Pour the sauce over the pudding and serve warm.

Raspberry Falooda

Makes 6–8

Ready in under 15 mins,
plus chilling

1 × 135g pack raspberry jelly

75g dried vermicelli pasta (such as
   angel hair pasta)

500ml just-boiled water from a
   kettle

100ml milk (ideally whole milk)

150ml double cream

25g caster sugar

½ tsp rose extract

200g fresh raspberries

400g good-quality vanilla ice cream

50g shelled pistachio nuts, roughly
   chopped, or flaked almonds

This is one of my favourite desserts – a grown-up version of
jelly and ice cream. The vermicelli might sound slightly odd in a
pudding, but along with the rose extract, it's what takes this from
the ordinary to the extraordinary. I think you'll love it!

Separate the jelly pieces and put them in a large microwaveable bowl
or jug – it will need to hold around 1 litre. Add 100ml cold water and cook
on HIGH for 1 min (1000W) 1 min 10 secs (800W), or until melted.

Stir in 500ml cold water and divide between 6 or 8 dessert dishes or tall
glass tumblers. Chill in the fridge for 6–8 hours, or until set. (This can be
prepared a day ahead.)

Snap the vermicelli pasta into small pieces, place in a large microwaveable
bowl and pour in the just-boiled water. Stir well to separate the strands.

Place the bowl on a large microwaveable plate, cover and cook on
HIGH for 3 mins (1000W), 3 mins 40 secs (800W), or until the pasta is
softened but retains a 'bite'.

Carefully drain the pasta in a large sieve and return to the bowl. Stir in the
milk, cream, sugar and rose extract. Cover and chill until you are ready to
assemble the pudding.

When ready to serve, take the jellies out of the fridge and divide the
creamy vermicelli between them. Top with the scoops of ice cream and
raspberries, then sprinkle with the nuts. Serve immediately.

Lime Cream Pie

Serves 8–10
Ready in under 20 mins,
plus overnight chilling

For the base and sides
85g butter, cubed
250g dark chocolate digestive
  biscuits

For the filling
juice of 1 lemon
finely grated zest of 4 limes and the
  juice of 2 limes
600ml double cream
150g caster sugar

I'm pretty sure this is the easiest pie you'll ever make. It has a crunchy chocolate biscuit base and a silky, creamy, lime filling. I sometimes serve it topped with a few fresh berries and a drizzle of single cream.

Line a 23cm tart tin with sloping sides or quiche dish with two layers of cling film, leaving some overhanging to help lift the pie out afterwards. (If using a ceramic dish that you are happy to serve the pie from, there is no need to line the dish, just grease with a little sunflower oil.)

To make the base, put the butter into a medium microwaveable bowl, cover and cook on HIGH for 30 secs (1000W), 40 secs (800W), or until melted.

Put the biscuits in a strong plastic food bag and bash into fine crumbs with the bottom of a saucepan (or blitz in a food processor); they shouldn't be too powdery. Add to the bowl with the melted butter and mix well.

Press the buttered crumbs firmly into the base and sides of the tin or dish with the back of a spoon until evenly covered, flattening the edges with your fingers. Put in the freezer for 30 mins.

Meanwhile, weigh the lemon juice, then add enough lime juice to make up to 70ml.

To make the filling, mix the cream and sugar in a large microwaveable mixing bowl or jug. Cover and cook on HIGH for 3 mins (1000W), 3 mins 40 secs (800W), or until the cream is hot but not boiling. Stir until the sugar dissolves.

Add the lime zest, followed by the lime and lemon juices, stirring for a few seconds, or just until the cream thickens a little. Pour the mixture carefully onto the prepared biscuit base. Cover and chill in the fridge for at least 8 hours or overnight until set.

Using the cling film to help you, gently lift the pie out of the tin or dish and carefully transfer to a serving plate. Cut into wedges and serve immediately.

Micro-tip —— Use unwaxed
limes, or scrub them well in warm water before grating. It's important to use the recommended amount of lime and lemon juice so the cream sets. For the most reliable results, weigh on digital scales.

Rhubarb and Elderflower Fool

Serves 6
Ready in under 10 mins,
plus chilling

500g young, slender rhubarb,
   trimmed and cut into roughly
   2.5cm lengths
3 tbsp elderflower cordial or water
115g caster sugar
200g ready-made custard
200g double cream

When it comes to rhubarb, the pinker the better! I'm slightly addicted to the fruit fools you can pick up in the supermarket but home-made tastes so much better and they are very easy to make. Mine is flavoured with elderflower, but you can make it with water or another kind of cordial instead.

Put the rhubarb in a large microwaveable bowl or wide-based casserole dish. If there are any thick stalks, cut them in half lengthways before slicing. Pour the cordial or water over the rhubarb, cover and cook on HIGH for 4 mins 50 secs (1000W), 6 mins (800W), or until very soft, stirring halfway.

Stir in the sugar and leave to cool for at least an hour.

Once the rhubarb is cold, spoon a third of the compote into a bowl and set aside.

Stir the custard into the remaining compote until well combined.

Whip the cream in a separate bowl until soft peaks form (you can use an electric mixer but don't let it get too stiff). Fold the cream gently into the rhubarb and custard mixture using a large metal spoon.

Spoon the reserved compote into individual dessert dishes or pretty glasses. Spoon the rhubarb and custard mixture on top, cover and chill in the fridge for at least 1 hour before serving.

Micro-tip —— You can make a gooseberry or blackcurrant fool in the same way. Keep the weights the same but be prepared to add more sugar.

If you are short of time, transfer the cooked rhubarb to a large shallow dish once the sugar is added and it will cool more quickly.

Best-ever Banoffee Pie

Serves 12
Ready in under 25 mins,
plus chilling

For the base and sides
85g butter, cubed
250g dark chocolate digestive
biscuits

For the filling
115g butter, cubed
115g soft dark brown sugar
1 × 397g can sweetened condensed
milk

For the topping
4 medium bananas
1 tsp lemon juice
300ml double cream, lightly
whipped
32g flaked chocolate bar or
equivalent, roughly broken

This is not just my best banoffee pie, but the easiest, too! Making the caramel in the microwave rather than boiling the condensed milk in the can for hours, is so much quicker and simpler.

Line a 20–23cm tart tin with sloping sides or quiche dish with two layers of cling film, leaving some overhanging to help lift the pie out afterwards. (If using a ceramic dish that you are happy to serve the pie from, there is no need to line the dish, just grease with a little sunflower oil.)

To make the base, put the butter into a medium microwaveable bowl, cover and cook on HIGH for 30 secs (1000W), 40 secs (800W), or until melted.

Put the biscuits in a strong plastic food bag and bash into fine crumbs with the bottom of a saucepan (or blitz to crumbs in a food processor). Add to the bowl with the melted butter and mix well.

Press the buttered crumbs firmly into the base and sides of the tin or dish with the back of a spoon until evenly covered, flattening the edge with your fingers. Put in the freezer for 30 mins.

To make the filling, put the butter, sugar and condensed milk into a large microwaveable bowl (it will need to be large enough for the caramel to rise as it boils). Cook on HIGH for 4 mins (1000W) or 5 mins (800W), stirring every minute. The caramel is ready when it has turned a creamy caramel brown and is fairly thick. Do not allow to overcook.

Taking care, as the bowl will be hot, pour the caramel carefully onto the biscuit base. Cool for 15 mins, then freeze for 1 hour.

Before serving, slice the bananas and toss with the lemon juice.

Use the cling film to gently lift the pie out of the tin or dish and carefully transfer to a serving plate. Scatter the bananas over the caramel, top with the whipped cream and sprinkle with the chocolate to finish.

Micro-tip —— If you don't
have a suitable tart tin, you can use a
20cm round, loose-based, shallow
cake tin instead (sandwich tin).

Rich Chocolate Mousse

Serves 6
Ready in under 10 mins,
plus chilling

190g dark chocolate (around
    55% cocoa solids), broken
    into chunks, plus extra grated
    chocolate, to serve
50g butter, cubed
6 eggs (medium or large), separated

A wonderfully old-fashioned, dead-simple chocolate mousse. The secret is to use a bog-standard dark chocolate, rather than a fancy one. It will taste rich without any of the bitterness you sometimes get with 70% cocoa chocolate. Make ahead if you like as it will keep well in the fridge for up to 3 days.

Put the chocolate pieces into a large microwaveable bowl, add the butter and cook uncovered on HIGH for 50 secs (1000W) or 1 min (800W), and stir.

Cook on HIGH for a further 30 secs (1000W or 800W – the cooking time won't vary much between wattages), and stir. Repeat, cooking at 20–30 second increments, if you need to, until the chocolate is almost fully melted. Take care as you melt the chocolate that it doesn't overcook and stiffen.

Stir until smooth then leave to cool for 30 mins.

Whisk the egg yolks in a separate bowl, then whisk them into the cooled chocolate.

In a clean bowl or stand mixer, whisk the egg whites until soft peaks form. Don't let them get too stiff or they will be difficult to combine with the chocolate mixture.

Take roughly a fifth of the egg white and gently fold into the chocolate mixture with a large metal spoon. This will make it easier for the rest of the egg white to be incorporated. Fold in the remainder all at once.

Spoon the mousse into individual dessert dishes, glass tumblers, or a serving bowl. Cover and leave to set in the fridge for at least 1½ hours before serving.

Sprinkle with a little extra chocolate and serve with cream, if you like.

Micro-tip —— This recipe contains raw eggs.

Apple and Blackberry Crumble

Serves 6
Ready in under 30 mins

100g caster sugar
finely grated zest of 1 small lemon
1 tsp ground cinnamon
800g cooking apples (ideally
    Bramley, around 4 medium
    apples), peeled, quartered,
    cored and chopped into small
    chunks
150g fresh or frozen blackberries

For the topping
100g butter, cubed
150g plain flour
100g demerara sugar
125g granola (ideally nutty granola)

Almost nothing beats a fruity crumble for a comforting weekend pudding. I've used apples and blackberries here but you can easily adapt this recipe for any fresh, frozen or canned fruit. Cooking in the microwave saves time and washing up!

Mix the caster sugar, lemon zest and cinnamon in a wide-based microwaveable pie dish (it will need to hold roughly 1.5 litres). Add the apple chunks and blackberries to the spiced sugar and toss well together.

Cover and cook on HIGH for 4 mins (1000W), 5 mins (800W), or until the blackberries are soft and juicy, stirring halfway. (If using frozen blackberries, you will need to increase the cooking time a little.)

While the fruit is cooking, make the topping. Rub the butter into the flour, sugar and granola until it resembles breadcrumbs, breaking up any large chunks of granola.

Sprinkle the topping over the cooked fruit and cook, uncovered, on HIGH for 5 mins (1000W), 6 mins 10 secs (800W), or until the topping is hot.

Micro-tip — Freeze
any leftovers for up to a month.
Thaw and reheat portions in the
microwave for 1–2 mins.

Lemon Possets

Serves 6
Ready in under 10 mins,
plus chilling overnight

575ml double cream
150g caster sugar
finely grated zest of 1 lemon and
    juice of 2–3 lemons (you'll need
    70ml juice), plus extra zest to
    serve
fresh raspberries, to serve

Probably the simplest dessert you'll ever make! A delicious,
lemony set cream. I serve my possets with the shortbread biscuits
on page 199, but any crisp, buttery biscuit would work perfectly.

Mix the cream and sugar in a large microwaveable mixing bowl or jug.
It will need to be large enough to hold at least 2 litres, in case the cream
rises as it heats.

Cover and cook on HIGH for 2 mins 50 secs (1000W), 3 mins 30 secs
(800W), or until the cream is hot. (It doesn't need to boil, but should be
heated enough to dissolve the sugar.)

Stir until the sugar dissolves, then add the zest of 1 lemon and all of the
juice. Continue stirring for 10–15 secs, or until the cream thickens slightly.

Divide the mixture between six ramekins, heat-proof tumblers or small
jars – they will each need to be large enough to hold around 125ml.

Cool for a few mins, then put the possets in the fridge for at least 6 hours
or overnight, until fully set.

Sprinkle with lemon zest and serve with fresh raspberries.

Micro-tip —— You'll need
to weigh the lemon juice to get
exactly the right amount to set the
cream. Ideally use unwaxed lemons,
or scrub them well under hot water
before finely grating.

Chocolate Sponge Puddings

Makes 4
Ready in under 15 mins

sunflower or vegetable oil,
    for greasing
100g butter, cubed
100g caster sugar
2 medium eggs
100g self-raising flour
25g cocoa powder, sifted
½ tsp baking powder

For the sauce
75g milk chocolate, broken
    into chunks
75ml double cream

These lovely little sponges with lashings of my easy milk chocolate sauce taste great. You could sprinkle some crushed chocolate honeycomb on top for an extra-special dessert.

Generously oil the insides of four 175ml microwaveable plastic or glass pudding basins or ramekins.

Put the butter in a large microwaveable bowl, separating the cubes a little. Cover and cook on HIGH for 20 secs (1000W), 30 secs (800W), or until softened but not melted.

Add the sugar, eggs, flour, cocoa powder and baking powder to the butter and beat until smooth and creamy. Spoon into the oiled dishes.

Place the dishes in a circle, spaced well apart, on the turntable or floor of the microwave and cook uncovered on HIGH for 3 mins (1000W), 3 mins 40 secs (800W), or until well risen and just firm to the touch. Leave to stand while the sauce is made.

Put the milk chocolate in a medium microwaveable bowl and add the cream. Cook on HIGH for 50 secs (1000W) or 1 min (800W), then stir until smooth.

Holding each pudding with a folded, dry tea towel in one hand, loosen the sides of the chocolate sponges with a round-ended knife and turn out onto individual small plates.

Spoon over the hot chocolate sauce and serve warm.

John's Spiced Plums

Serves 4
Ready in under 10 mins

600g plums (around 12)
4 tbsp orange juice, fresh or from a carton
3 tbsp caster sugar, or to taste
4 star anise
½ tsp ground cinnamon

I almost didn't put this poached fruit recipe in the book but it's such a handy dessert and is incredibly simple, so it seemed a shame not to share it with you. I like to make it with plums, but it also works well with pears or apples, although you will need to tweak the cooking time a little.

Cut the plums in half and remove the stones.

Place the fruit in a wide-based microwaveable dish (any stubborn stones can be more easily removed once they are cooked). Sprinkle with the orange juice, sugar, star anise and cinnamon, and stir lightly. Cover and cook on HIGH for 4 mins (1000W) or 5 mins (800W).

Stir gently, then cover and cook on HIGH for 2 mins (1000W), 2 mins 30 secs (800W), or until the plums are just tender.

Remove the star anise and serve the plums hot or cold with lightly whipped cream, pouring cream or ice cream. They are also delicious with custard (page 215).

Micro-tip —— For an extra-special dessert, serve with whipped cream and lightly crushed amaretti biscuits.

Raspberry Bakewell Pudding

Serves 4–6
Ready in under 25 mins

A lovely almondy pudding, with a layer of peach jam and fresh raspberries – a bit like a Bakewell tart but without the pastry. Serve with cream or clotted cream.

sunflower or vegetable oil, for greasing
150g raspberry jam
125g butter, cubed
125g caster sugar
75g ground almonds
2 large eggs
100g self-raising flour
1 tsp almond or vanilla extract
100g fresh raspberries
25g toasted flaked almonds
icing sugar, sifted, to serve (optional)

Lightly oil the base and sides of a shallow 23cm microwaveable dish. Spoon the jam into the dish and spread out with a spatula or the back of a spoon.

Put the butter in a large microwaveable bowl, separating the cubes a little. Cover and cook on HIGH for 20 secs (1000W) or 30 secs (800W), until softened but not melted.

Add the sugar, ground almonds, eggs, flour and almond or vanilla extract and beat with a whisk or wooden spoon until pale and creamy.

Drop large spoonfuls of the almond mixture on top of the jam.

Dot with the raspberries, pushing them in lightly. Cook on HIGH for 4 mins 50 secs (1000W) or 6 mins (800W).

Sprinkle with the flaked almonds and cook on HIGH for 1 min 30 secs (1000W), 2 mins (800W), or until the pudding is well risen and firm to the touch.

Sprinkle with a little sifted icing sugar to serve, if you like.

Strawberry Meringue Cream

Serves 6
Ready in under 10 mins,
plus cooling and chilling

500g fresh strawberries, hulled and
    roughly chopped, plus a few
    extra to serve
10g powdered gelatine
75g caster sugar
100g full-fat Greek yoghurt
300ml double cream, lightly
    whipped
6–8 ready-made meringues,
    roughly broken
1 tsp freeze-dried strawberry or
    raspberry pieces, to decorate
    (optional)

A really easy, light dessert that makes the most of ripe summer
strawberries and tastes so much better than the shop-bought kind.

Tip the strawberries into a microwaveable bowl – it needs to be large
enough to add all the other ingredients later – and pour 3 tbsp of cold
water over the berries. Cook uncovered on HIGH for 3 mins (1000W),
3 mins 40 secs (800W), or until very soft, stirring halfway. Use a potato
masher to crush the strawberries and release their juice.

Whisk the gelatine into the softened berries a little at a time.

Whisk in the sugar, cover loosely and leave to cool at room temperature
for about 1 hour.

Stir in the yoghurt until well combined.

Gently fold the lightly whipped cream into the strawberry and yoghurt
mixture using a large metal spoon.

Divide between individual dessert dishes or glass tumblers, or spoon
into a large glass trifle bowl. Cover tightly and leave to set in the fridge
for several hours or overnight.

Decorate with crushed meringues and freeze-dried strawberry or
raspberry pieces, if using, just before serving.

Micro-tip —— This is a
great recipe for using up berries
that are past their best – just avoid
any that are obviously mouldy.

CAKES & COOKIES

Cinnamon Apple Cake

Makes 9 squares
Ready in under 20 mins

A fantastic cake that works just as well at coffee time as it does as a quick pudding. It's a bit like a warm apple strudel in cake form, so feel free to serve it with cream or custard, if you like!

For the cake

sunflower or vegetable oil, for
    greasing
100g butter, cubed
3 medium eggs
100g caster sugar
150g self-raising flour
½ tsp baking powder
1½ tsp vanilla extract
80g sultanas

For the topping

400g cooking apples (around
    2 medium apples), peeled,
    quartered, cored and thinly sliced
2 tbsp caster sugar
1 tsp ground cinnamon
icing sugar, to serve (optional)

Lightly oil the inside of a roughly 20cm square microwaveable dish. Line the base with a wide strip of non-stick baking paper so that two opposite sides are long enough to rise about 4cm above the rim of the dish – this will make it easier to lift the cake out once it is 'baked'.

Put the butter in a large microwaveable bowl, cover and cook on HIGH for 20 secs (1000W), 30 secs (800W), or until softened but not melted.

Put the remaining cake ingredients, except the sultanas, in the bowl with the butter and beat hard with a wooden spoon until smooth and creamy (you can use an electric mixer, if you prefer).

Spoon into the prepared dish and sprinkle the sultanas over the top.

Put the apple slices in a large bowl and toss with the sugar and cinnamon.

Arrange the spiced apple slices over the cake batter. Cook uncovered on HIGH for 7 mins (1000W), 8 mins 40 secs (800W), or until the cake is risen and firm, and the apples are soft. It may still look a little moist but it shouldn't be too wet – if it is, return it to the microwave for another minute or so. Leave to stand for 5 mins.

Serve warm or cold, dusted with icing sugar, if you like.

Micro-tip —— You will need a roughly 20cm square microwaveable dish – a Pyrex one is ideal. If using a different shape, you will need to tweak the cooking times a little.

Strawberry Cream Sponge

Serves 10–12
Ready in under 20 mins,
plus cooling

sunflower or vegetable oil, for
    greasing
175g butter, cubed
175g caster sugar, plus 2 tbsp
3 large eggs
200g self-raising flour
½ tsp baking powder
1 tsp vanilla extract
icing sugar, for dusting

For the filling

125g strawberry jam
100ml double cream, whipped until
    soft peaks form
100g fresh strawberries, hulled
    and sliced

A glamorous, light and summery cake that works as a sumptuous dessert or a treat at tea time. It's a real show-stopper! And no one will believe you 'baked' it in the microwave.

Lightly oil the inside of two 20cm round silicone cake moulds. Line the bases with non-stick baking paper.

Put the butter in a large microwaveable mixing bowl and separate the cubes slightly. Cook uncovered on HIGH for 20 secs (1000W), 30 secs (800W), or until softened but not melted.

Add 175g caster sugar, eggs, flour, baking powder and vanilla extract, and beat with a wooden spoon or an electric mixer until well combined, thick and creamy.

Spoon evenly into the prepared moulds and smooth the surface. Cook one sponge at a time uncovered on HIGH for 3 mins (1000W), 3 mins 40 secs (800W), or until the sponge is well risen and just firm to the touch. Leave to stand in the microwave for 5 mins; it will continue cooking for a short while.

Meanwhile, cover a cooling rack with a sheet of non-stick baking paper and sprinkle with 2 tbsp caster sugar.

Turn the cake out onto the sugared paper, remove the mould and lining paper and leave to cool. Make the second sponge in the same way.

To assemble the cake, place one of the sponges on a serving plate or cake stand and spread with the jam without taking it right to the edges. Spoon the cream over the jam and spread gently. Scatter over the strawberries, then sandwich the second sponge on top. Dust with sifted icing sugar to serve.

Micro-tip —— You can leave out the cream and fresh strawberries for a more simple cake, if you prefer.

Fastest Fruit Cake

Serves 12
Ready in under 30 mins,
plus cooling

500g luxury mixed dried fruit

finely grated zest and juice of 1
lemon

100ml orange juice (fresh or from a
carton)

sunflower or vegetable oil, for
greasing

150g butter, cubed

150g soft dark brown sugar

3 large eggs

175g plain flour

50g ground almonds

2 tsp ground mixed spice

caster sugar, for dusting
(optional)

If you love fruit cake but don't want to wait more than an hour
for it to bake, this could be the answer. Cooked in under 15 mins,
it's packed with plump dried fruit and just the right amount of spice.

Put the dried fruit, lemon zest and juice, and the orange juice in a large
microwaveable bowl. Cover and cook on HIGH for 4 mins (1000W) or
5 mins (800W), stirring halfway. Leave to cool. (Heating the fruit in this
way will make it extra plump – if you spread the hot fruit over a baking
tray, it will cool more quickly.)

Grease a 23cm silicone cake mould (see Micro-tip) with oil and line
the base with a circle of non-stick baking paper.

To make the cake, put the butter in a large microwaveable mixing bowl
and spread the cubes slightly apart. Cook uncovered on HIGH for
20 secs (1000W), 30 secs (800W), or until softened but not melted.

Add the sugar, eggs, flour, ground almonds and mixed spice and beat
with a wooden spoon or an electric mixer until well combined and thick
and creamy looking.

Stir in the soaked fruit until thoroughly combined.

Spoon into the prepared mould and smooth the surface. Cook on HIGH
for 10 mins (1000W), 12 mins (800W), or until the cake is slightly risen
and firm to the touch. It will continue cooking as it stands but if it is
looking extremely wet around the edges or middle, cook for 1–2 mins
longer. Leave to cool in the mould.

Turn out onto a plate or board and sprinkle with caster sugar, if using,
to serve.

Micro-tip —— You could
use a ceramic or toughened glass
dish instead of a silicone cake
mould but you will need to adjust
the cooking time a little.

Sticky Ginger Cake

Serves 10
Ready in under 20 mins,
plus cooling

sunflower or vegetable oil, for
    greasing
115g self-raising flour
1 tsp bicarbonate of soda
3 tsp ground ginger
1 tsp ground cinnamon
80g butter, cubed
80g dark brown soft sugar
45g black treacle
45g golden syrup
80ml milk
2 medium eggs

For the icing
115g icing sugar
3 balls stem ginger (from a jar),
    diced

)))

Micro-tip —— If you
like baking, it's worth investing in a
silicone loaf mould (see page 220);
you'll find plenty of choice online.
You can use a ceramic or toughened
glass loaf pan, but you will need to
tweak the cooking time.

This cake is gorgeous topped with a jewelled ginger icing, or it can
be eaten warm, fresh from the oven, with custard or cream. It keeps
extremely well for 2–3 days, if wrapped in foil.

Lightly oil the inside of a 22cm silicone loaf mould. Line the base and
sides with non-stick baking paper. Cut the lining paper so that two of the
opposite sides are long enough to rise about 4cm above the rim of the
dish – this will make it easier to lift the cake out once it's 'baked'. (You
can also use a non-stick loaf liner.)

Put the flour, bicarbonate of soda and spices in a large microwaveable
bowl and mix well.

In a separate medium microwaveable bowl, add the butter, sugar,
treacle and syrup. Cook uncovered for 2 mins (1000W), 2 mins 30 secs
(800W), or until melted, stirring after 1 min 30 secs.

Stir the milk into the treacle mixture, then add the eggs and whisk until
well combined.

Make a well in the centre of the flour mixture, then slowly pour the
treacle mixture into the flour, whisking to form a smooth batter.

Pour the cake batter into the prepared mould and place in the centre
of the microwave. Cook on HIGH for 4 mins (1000W), 5 mins (800W),
or until the cake is well risen, firm to the touch and a skewer inserted
into the centre comes out clean. Leave to cool in the mould for at least
30 mins.

Turn the cake out onto a board, peel off the lining paper and leave to cool.

Sift the icing sugar into a bowl and stir in enough cold water to make
a fairly thick, smooth icing (around 4–5 tsp). Drizzle the icing over the
cake, then sprinkle with the ginger pieces.

Leave to stand for 30 mins before serving.

Easy Vanilla Cupcakes

Makes 4
Ready in under 20 mins,
plus cooling

50g butter, cubed
50g caster sugar
1 medium egg
½ tsp vanilla extract
50g self-raising flour
¼ tsp baking powder

For the icing
100g butter, cubed
1 tsp vanilla extract
1 tsp milk
200g icing sugar
1 tsp freeze-dried raspberry
    or strawberry pieces,
    to decorate (optional)

A fab recipe to make with children as the results are almost instantaneous. These light sponge cakes with creamy butter icing can be decorated any way you like.

Line four medium ramekin dishes (around 8cm diameter) with paper cupcake cases. If you don't have ramekin dishes, you can place the cases in microwaveable cups or mugs instead.

Put the butter for the cakes in a large microwaveable mixing bowl and cook on HIGH for 10 secs (1000W), 15 secs (800W), or until softened but not melted.

Add the sugar, egg, vanilla extract, flour and baking powder and beat with a wooden spoon or whisk until smooth and creamy. Divide between the cupcake cases as evenly as you can (you can weigh the mixture, if you like).

Place the ramekins in a circle, spaced well apart, on the turntable or the floor of the microwave. Cook uncovered on HIGH for 2 mins (1000W), 2 mins 30 secs (800W), or until risen and just firm to the touch. They should still look just slightly damp around the edges, so don't be tempted to overcook them.

Leave the cupcakes to stand for 5 minutes before removing from the microwave. Turn out onto a wire rack, flip the right side up and leave to cool.

To make the icing, place the butter in a large microwaveable bowl, and cook on HIGH for 20 secs (1000W), 30 secs (800W), or until softened but not melted.

Add the vanilla extract and milk, then sift the icing sugar on top. Beat hard with a wooden spoon until smooth and fluffy, or use an electric whisk.

Either spoon or pipe onto the cakes, decorate with freeze-dried raspberry or strawberry pieces, if using, and serve.

Micro-tip —— For really easy syrup sponge puddings, turn the just-cooked cakes out onto small plates or bowls and peel off the paper cases. Warm some golden syrup in a bowl in the microwave for a few secs then pour over the sponges to serve.

Lemon Drizzle Cake

Serves 10
Ready in under 25 mins,
plus cooling

sunflower or vegetable oil, for
    greasing
115g butter, cubed
115g caster sugar
2 medium eggs
140g self-raising flour
¼ tsp baking powder
finely grated zest of 2 large lemons

For the lemon syrup topping
50g caster sugar
juice of 2 large lemons (around
    75ml)

Lemon drizzle cake is one of my favourites and is incredibly easy to make in the microwave. Even if you aren't a confident baker, give it a go. The golden caster sugar brings a rich colour to the cake.

Lightly oil the inside of a 22cm silicone loaf mould. Line the base and sides with non-stick baking paper. Cut the lining paper so that two of the opposite sides are long enough to rise about 4cm above the rim of the dish – this will make it easier to lift the cake out once it's baked. (You can also use a non-stick paper loaf tin liner.)

Put the butter in a large microwaveable mixing bowl and separate the cubes slightly. Cook uncovered on HIGH for 20 secs (1000W), 30 secs (800W), or until softened but not melted.

Add the sugar, eggs, flour, baking powder and lemon zest. Beat with a wooden spoon or an electric mixer until well combined, thick and creamy.

Spoon into the prepared dish and smooth the surface. Cook uncovered on HIGH for 3 mins 10 secs (1000W), 4 mins (800W), or until the cake is well risen and just firm to the touch. A skewer inserted into the centre of the cake should come out clean.

Leave to cool for 30 mins, then lift out of the mould and place on a platter or board. Gently remove the lining paper.

To make the topping, set aside 1½ tbsp of the caster sugar and mix the remaining sugar with the lemon juice.

Pour the lemon syrup slowly over the cake (there is no need to prick the surface of the cake first). Leave to soak in for a few mins, then sprinkle with the reserved sugar and leave to cool for at least 1 hour before serving.

Quickest Banana Loaf

Serves 10
Ready in under 20 mins,
plus cooling

sunflower or vegetable oil, for
    greasing
2 ripe medium bananas (around
    175g peeled weight)
85g butter, cubed
2 large eggs
70g soft light brown sugar
175g self-raising flour
1 tsp ground mixed spice
½ tsp baking powder

For the topping
100g Caramilk chocolate buttons
40g dried banana chips, roughly
    broken
40g pecan nuts, roughly broken

))))

Micro-tips —— If you like
baking, it's worth investing in a
silicone loaf mould: you'll find plenty
of choice online. You can use a
ceramic or toughened glass loaf
pan, but you may need to tweak
the cooking time.

Use milk or dark chocolate buttons
instead, if you like.

A brilliantly quick banana loaf that is the perfect way to use up over-ripe bananas. You can serve this warm, or leave to cool and ice with my crunchy caramel topping.

Lightly oil the inside of a 22cm silicone loaf mould. Line the base with non-stick baking paper. Cut the lining paper so that two of the opposite sides are long enough to rise about 4cm above the rim of the dish – this will make it easier to lift the cake out once it's cooked. (You can also use a non-stick paper loaf tin liner if you like.)

Put the bananas on a plate and mash thoroughly with a fork.

Put the butter in a large microwaveable mixing bowl, cover and cook on HIGH for 40 secs (1000W), 50 secs (800W), or until melted.

Put the mashed bananas in the bowl with the melted butter. Add the eggs and sugar and whisk together well.

Add the flour, spice and baking powder and whisk or beat together until thoroughly combined.

Pour into the prepared loaf tin and cook uncovered on HIGH for 6 mins 30 secs (1000W), 8 mins (800W), or until the cake is well risen and firm to the touch. A skewer inserted into the centre should come out clean.

Leave to stand for 10 mins, then lift out onto a wire rack, peel off the lining paper and leave to cool.

To make the topping, put the chocolate in a medium microwaveable bowl and cook uncovered for 50 secs (1000W) or 1 min (800W). Leave to stand for 3 mins, then stir until smooth.

Drizzle the chocolate over the cake, then sprinkle with the banana chips and pecan nuts. Leave to set before slicing.

Caramel Crispies

Makes 20 squares
Ready in under 10 mins,
plus chilling

sunflower or vegetable oil, for
    greasing
100g butter, cubed
6 Mars Bars or equivalent (around
    236g total weight), sliced
115g puffed rice

For the topping (optional)
100g white chocolate buttons or
    drops
100g dark or milk chocolate buttons
    or drops

This always goes down well with kids and can be made with or without the chocolate topping. It will last well for about a week, so serve in small squares as an occasional treat or at parties.

Lightly oil the inside of a shallow, 20cm square cake tin. Line the base with non-stick baking paper. Cut the lining paper so that two of the opposite sides are long enough to rise about 4cm above the rim of the dish – this will make it easier to lift the 'bake' out once it is ready.

Put the butter and sliced Mars Bars or equivalent in a large microwaveable bowl and cook uncovered on HIGH for 1 min (1000W) or 1 min 10 secs (800W). Stir well, then cook uncovered on HIGH for 30 secs (1000W), 40 secs (800W), or until almost melted.

Stir vigorously with a wooden spoon until the sauce is smooth and fully melted. It may look a little oily to begin with but will come together as you stir.

Add the puffed rice and stir until thoroughly combined. Tip into the prepared tin and press firmly into the base and corners with the back of a metal spoon (a wooden spoon will stick).

Put the chocolate buttons or drops in separate microwaveable bowls and cook uncovered on HIGH for 40 secs (1000W), 50 secs (800W), or until the chocolate softens. Leave to stand for 3 mins, then stir until smooth.

Drizzle over the crispies, then use a skewer or the end of a teaspoon to swirl the chocolate topping. Leave to cool for 30 mins, then place in the fridge for 1–2 hours, or until set.

Cut into squares to serve.

Rich Chocolate Brownies

Makes 6–12
Ready in under 20 mins

Fantastic served warm and gooey at coffee or tea time, or as a dessert with vanilla ice cream. You'll have six generous bars as a pudding or 12 small squares.

sunflower or vegetable oil, for
    greasing
100g butter, cubed
100g caster sugar
2 medium eggs
40g plain flour
25g cocoa powder
65g dark (around 55% cocoa solids)
    or milk chocolate, roughly
    chopped into 1cm pieces
icing sugar, to serve (optional)

Lightly oil the inside of a 22cm silicone loaf mould. Line the base with non-stick baking paper. Cut the lining paper so that two of the opposite sides are long enough to rise about 4cm above the rim of the dish – this will make it easier to lift the cake out once it's baked. You can also use a non-stick paper loaf tin liner if you like.

Put the butter and sugar in a large microwaveable mixing bowl. Cover and cook on HIGH for 50 secs (1000W), 1 min (800W), or until the butter is melted.

Beat with a large whisk for 1–2 mins, until the sugar dissolves and the mixture looks smooth and glossy. Add the eggs and whisk until smooth.

Sift the flour and cocoa powder on top of the mixture. Whisk until thoroughly combined, then pour into the prepared dish.

Scatter the chocolate pieces over the cake batter and cook on HIGH for 2 mins 40 secs (1000W), 3 mins 10 secs (800W), or until the brownie is risen and just firm to the touch. It will still look a little moist in places but that's fine.

Leave to stand for 5 mins, then lift out onto a board and cut into 6 bars to serve warm, or allow to cool and cut into 12 small squares. Dust with sifted icing sugar to serve, if you like.

Micro-tip —— If you like baking, it's worth investing in a silicone loaf mould: you'll find plenty of choice online. You can also use a ceramic or toughened glass loaf pan, but you will need to tweak the cooking time.

Oaty Chewy Cookies

Makes 12
Ready in under 15 mins,
plus cooling

75g butter, cubed
50g soft light brown sugar
1 tbsp golden syrup
115g porridge oats (not jumbo)

A great recipe to make with kids, as these chewy biscuits cook
so quickly. Delicious with a cup of tea.

Line three large microwaveable plates with circles of non-stick baking
paper.

Stir the butter, sugar and syrup together in a large microwaveable bowl.
Cover and cook on HIGH for 50 secs (1000W) or 1 min (800W). Stir until
smooth.

Add the oats and stir until the mixture comes together in damp clumps.

Place four mounds, each around 20g, on each of the plates, spaced well
apart in a circle to allow them to spread. Cook uncovered, one plate
at a time, on HIGH for 40 secs (1000W), 50 secs (800W), or until the
biscuits look lacey but not browned. Don't let them over cook.

Leave to cool on their plates until firm, then slide onto a wire rack to
finish cooling and crisp up before removing from the paper.

Micro-tip —— Depending on
your oven, these cookies could take
longer to cook. They will be quite flat
and lacey-looking when ready.

Coconut and Chocolate Tiffin

Makes 36 squares
Ready in under 10 mins,
plus chilling

sunflower or vegetable oil, for
    greasing
100g coconut oil
75g golden syrup
150g dark chocolate (around 70%
    cocoa solids), broken into chunks
150g milk chocolate, broken into
    chunks
100g mixed dried fruit (including
    cranberries and apricots)
75g desiccated coconut, plus 3 tbsp
    for sprinkling
200g caramelised or digestive
    biscuits, broken into small pieces

A sweet, indulgent treat that goes perfectly with a strong cup
of coffee or tea. I use caramelised biscuits, such as Biscoff, but
digestives, rich tea or any other kind of biscuit would work well.
Just break the biscuits into small pieces with your fingers – there's
no need to crush them completely.

Lightly oil a 20cm square, loose-bottomed cake tin and line the base
with non-stick baking paper. (If your tin isn't loose-based, cut the lining
paper so that two of the opposite sides are long enough to rise about
4cm above the rim of the dish – this will make it easier to lift the tiffin out
once it's set.)

Put the coconut oil and syrup in a large microwaveable mixing bowl.
You'll need a large bowl as the rest of the ingredients are going to be
added later. Cook uncovered on HIGH for 1 min (1000W) or 1 min 10
secs (800W), until melted.

Stir in both the chocolates and cook uncovered on HIGH for 1 min
(1000W) or 1 min 10 secs (800W). Stir well until the mixture comes
together to make a smooth, glossy sauce.

Stir in the dried fruit and 75g of the coconut, followed by the biscuits.
Spoon into the prepared tin, and flatten the surface with a spatula or
palette knife.

Sprinkle with the remaining coconut and chill in the fridge for several
hours, or overnight.

Lift out of the tin, remove the baking paper and cut into small squares
to serve. They'll keep well in a lidded container in the fridge for up to
a week.

Micro-tip —— You can use
any dried fruit for this recipe, but luxury
dried fruit with added apricots and
cranberries is particularly delicious.
Otherwise, simple raisins or sultanas
work well – and you can swap some
fruit for nuts, if you prefer.

Shortbread Biscuits

Makes 8
Ready in under 15 mins,
plus cooling

50g butter, cubed
25g golden caster sugar, plus extra
    for sprinkling
75g plain flour

Gorgeous served with a hot cup of tea or as a lovely accompaniment to desserts, such as the Lemon Possets (page 164) or Rich Chocolate Mousse (page 160). If you want to make more biscuits, simply increase the quantities, but always cook just four at a time for the most reliable results.

Line two large microwaveable plates with circles of non-stick baking paper.

Put the butter in a medium microwaveable bowl and spread the cubes slightly apart. Cover and cook on HIGH for 20 secs (1000W), 25 secs (800W), or until just melted.

Stir in the sugar and flour and mix with a wooden spoon until the dough forms a ball.

Divide the dough into eight equal pieces and roll each one into a small ball. Place four balls on each of the plates, spaced well apart in a circle. Flatten a little with your fingertips until around 1cm thick.

Cook uncovered, one plate at time, on HIGH for 1 min 20 secs (1000W), 1 min 40 secs (800W), or until the biscuits look firm and dry at the edges. They will still be a little soft but shouldn't look brown. If there are brown areas (check inside the biscuits for browning, too), reduce the cooking time for the next batch by a few seconds.

Slide the paper onto a wire rack, sprinkle the biscuits with a little extra sugar, and leave to cool and crisp up before removing from the paper.

Stored in an airtight container, they will last for several days.

Micro-tip —— You can also place the cooled biscuits on a sheet of baking paper and drizzle with chocolate that has been melted in the microwave for a few secs. Leave to set.

SAUCES & TOPPINGS

Basic White Sauce

Makes 350ml
Ready in under 10 mins

35g butter, cubed
35g plain flour
350ml milk

If you've always ended up with lumpy or disappointing results when you've attempted a white sauce in the past, give this recipe a go. Easy and versatile, and so much cheaper than shop-bought, too.

Put the butter in a large microwaveable bowl. Cook uncovered on HIGH for 20 secs (1000W), 30 secs (800W), or until melted.

Stir in the flour, then whisk in the milk, a good pinch of salt and a little ground black or white pepper.

Cover and cook on HIGH for 5 mins (1000W) or 6 mins (800W), whisking after 2 mins and then every min, until the sauce is smooth and thick.

Add a little more salt or pepper, to taste, if needed.

Micro-tip —— Add 50g finely grated mature Cheddar to make a cheese sauce – perfect with cooked veg or pasta. Adding chopped fresh parsley instead of cheese makes a great sauce for fish and adding a couple of teaspoons of mustard makes a fab sauce for gammon.

Cheat's Hollandaise

Serves 4
Ready in under 10 mins

2 large egg yolks
1½ tsp white wine vinegar
½ tsp Dijon mustard
pinch of caster sugar
150g butter, cubed

Home-made hollandaise can be unpredictable but with this straightforward recipe, you'll achieve fantastic results every time. I like to serve it over poached eggs for breakfast (page 25), or spooned onto freshly cooked asparagus for lunch. Stir in some freshly chopped tarragon at the end and you'll have a brilliant sauce for steak, too.

Whisk the egg yolks, vinegar, mustard and sugar in a medium microwaveable mixing bowl, and season with salt and lots of ground black pepper. Use a large whisk, not a fork, so the yolks are thoroughly combined.

Put the butter in a microwaveable jug, cover and cook on HIGH for 1 min (1000W) or 1 min 10 secs (800W), until melted.

Pour the hot butter in a thin, steady steam into the egg mixture, whisking constantly. When all the butter is combined, cook the sauce uncovered on HIGH for 20 secs (1000W/800W), then whisk well.

Cook on HIGH for 20 secs (1000W/800W) and whisk again. The cooking increments are so short here that you don't need to change depending on the wattage of your machine.

Finally, cook on HIGH for 10 secs (1000W/800W) and whisk again. The sauce should be just thickened and the whisk should leave a trail when lifted from the sauce. It will continue to cook for a short while, so don't overcook or the eggs may scramble.

Adjust the seasoning to taste and serve.

Simple Tomato Pasta Sauce

Serves 4
Ready in under 15 mins

1 medium onion, peeled and finely
    chopped

2 garlic cloves, peeled and crushed

3 tbsp extra-virgin olive or sunflower
    oil

1 × 400g can chopped tomatoes

2 tbsp tomato purée

½ tsp caster sugar

½ tsp dried oregano or Italian herbs

¼–½ tsp dried chilli flakes (optional)

A basic tomato sauce that's ready in under 15 mins. It's a great one to make if you are a novice in the kitchen, as there is very little to go wrong. Add a generous pinch of chilli for an arrabbiata-style sauce. Serve with freshly cooked pasta or as a sauce for grilled meats, fish or vegetables.

Mix the onion, garlic and oil in a large microwaveable bowl or dish. Season with salt and ground black pepper and toss together well. Cover and cook on HIGH for 5 mins (1000W), 6 mins 10 secs (800W), or until softened, stirring halfway.

Stir in the tomatoes, tomato purée, sugar, oregano or Italian herbs and chilli flakes, if using. Cover and cook on HIGH for 4 mins (1000W) or 5 mins (800W), stirring halfway.

Check the seasoning before serving.

Micro-tips —— For a smoother sauce, blitz with a stick blender.

Stir in roughly 3 tbsp finely shredded basil at the end of the cooking time, if you like, or add a handful of sliced pitted olives and some capers with the tomatoes for a puttanesca-style sauce.

Fresh Cherry Tomato and Basil Sauce

Serves 2
Ready in under 10 mins

250g cherry tomatoes, halved
1 garlic clove, peeled and crushed
3 tbsp extra-virgin olive oil
½ tsp caster sugar
small bunch of fresh basil (around
    6–7 leaves), finely shredded

A punchy tomato and fragrant basil sauce that's perfect tossed through pasta and makes a great topping for bruschetta. If you don't have any cherry tomatoes handy, you can roughly chop any fresh, ripe tomatoes instead.

Put the tomatoes into a microwaveable bowl. Cover and cook on HIGH for 3 mins (1000W) or 3 mins 40 secs (800W).

Stir in the garlic, oil, sugar, a good pinch of salt and a few twists of ground black pepper. Cover and cook on HIGH for 1 min 40 secs (1000W), 2 mins (800W), or until the tomatoes are soft but still holding their shape.

Stir in the basil and serve.

Micro-tip —— Stir in a generous pinch of dried chilli flakes at the same time as the garlic, if you like a more fiery flavour.

Creamy Mushroom Sauce

Serves 4
Ready in under 15 mins

½ medium onion, peeled and finely
    chopped
150g small chestnut mushrooms,
    sliced
1 tbsp sunflower or vegetable oil
1 garlic clove, peeled and crushed
1 tbsp plain flour
2 tbsp white wine or water
150ml double cream

A brilliant sauce to serve with any cooked meat or fish, and great with nut loaf or over griddled vegetables. Add a few more mushrooms and pinch of paprika for a fab stroganoff-style dish for two.

Stir the onion, mushrooms, oil and garlic together in a medium microwaveable bowl. Cover and cook on HIGH for 5 mins (1000W) or 6 mins 10 secs (800W), stirring halfway.

Stir in the flour followed by the wine or water and cream. Season with a little salt and lots of ground black pepper. Cover and cook on HIGH for 3 mins 10 secs (1000W), 4 mins (800W), or until hot, stirring halfway.

Adjust the seasoning to taste.

Creamy Peppercorn Sauce

Serves 4
Ready in under 15 mins

1 tbsp black peppercorns

25g butter, cubed

½ small onion or 1 long shallot, peeled and finely chopped

1 garlic clove, peeled and crushed

small sprig of fresh thyme or pinch of dried thyme

1 tbsp plain flour

2 tbsp brandy

125ml hot beef stock (made with ½ stock cube, preferably Oxo)

100ml double cream

There'll be no more mixing packets or buying tubs of ready-made sauce once you've tasted my version of a peppercorn sauce. Fantastic with steak or poured over griddled tuna, it has just the right amount of fiery black pepper, tempered with lashings of silky cream.

Put the peppercorns in a pestle and mortar and bash until they are coarsely crushed. You can also blitz in a spice grinder but don't let them get too finely ground; they need to have a bit of bite. Set aside.

Put the butter, onion or shallot, garlic and thyme in a medium microwaveable bowl. Cover and cook on HIGH for 4 mins (1000W) or 5 mins (800W), stirring halfway.

Remove the fresh thyme, if using.

Stir in the flour, then the peppercorns, brandy, stock and cream. Cover and cook on HIGH for 2 mins 30 secs (1000W) or 3 mins (800W), stirring halfway.

Add a little salt, to taste, and serve warm.

Micro-tip —— The sauce can be prepared ahead and warmed through in the microwave for 1–2 minutes before serving, if you like.

If you are serving with pan-fried steak, add the sauce to the pan while the steaks are resting and simmer for a few seconds, stirring in the cooking juices.

Really Good Cheese Sauce

Makes around 400ml
Ready in under 10 mins

35g butter, cubed

35g plain flour

350ml milk

75g mature Cheddar, or a mixture of
cheeses, finely grated

1 tsp English mustard

Making roux-style sauces in the microwave is a cinch. You just need to arm yourself with a metal whisk and you are guaranteed silky, lump-free results. This easy, cheesy sauce is perfect poured over cooked veg, tossed through cooked pasta and layered into lasagne.

Put the butter in a large microwaveable bowl. Cook uncovered on HIGH for 20 secs (1000W), 30 secs (800W), or until melted.

Stir in the flour, then whisk in the milk, a good pinch of salt and a little ground black pepper. Cover and cook on HIGH for 2 mins (1000W) or 2 mins 30 secs (800W).

Whisk in the cheese and mustard. Cover and cook on HIGH for 3 mins 40 secs (1000W) or 4 mins (800W), whisking every minute until the sauce is smooth and thick and doesn't taste at all 'floury'.

Add a little more salt or pepper to taste.

Rich Chicken Gravy

Serves 4–5
Ready in under 10 mins

350ml hot chicken stock (made with
    1 stock cube)

2 tbsp white wine

1 rasher smoked bacon, roughly
    chopped

1 tbsp redcurrant jelly

1 tsp yeast extract, such as Marmite

2 tbsp cornflour mixed with 2 tbsp
    cold water

People often ask me how they can make a decent gravy without resorting to granules and I'm happy to say that this is the answer. If you swap the chicken stock cube for lamb or beef and omit the bacon, you'll also have a good gravy for other meats. Add meat juices from the roast and it will taste even better.

Put the stock, wine, bacon, redcurrant jelly and Marmite or gravy browning in a large microwaveable jug or bowl. Season with ground black pepper and stir well.

Stir in the cornflour mixture, cover and cook on HIGH for 3 mins 10 secs (1000W) or 4 mins (800W), stirring halfway, until smooth and thickened.

Strain through a sieve into a warmed gravy jug, check the seasoning and serve.

Easiest Mashed Potatoes

Serves 4
Ready in under 20 mins

4 medium floury potatoes (around 750g total weight), preferably Maris Piper
50g butter, cubed
150ml milk
3–4 tbsp cream (optional)

The fluffiest, creamiest mash – and it's made in the microwave! Use for topping fish or cottage pies, or as a cosy accompaniment to casseroles and grilled or roast meats.

Prick the potatoes 4–5 times all over with a fork. Place on a large microwaveable plate lined with plain, microwave-safe kitchen paper (not recycled – see page 223), spaced apart.

Cook uncovered on HIGH for about 12 minutes (1000W), 15 mins (800W), turning over every 4–5 minutes, or until they feel soft if you squeeze them. If there are hard areas, turn them over again and cook for a further 1–2 minutes.

Cut the potatoes in half and, holding each half with folded kitchen paper or a dry cloth as they will be hot, use a dessert spoon to scoop out the cooked potato and place it in a bowl. Discard the skins.

Add the butter, milk and cream, if using, to the bowl and season generously with salt and ground black pepper. Cover and cook on HIGH for 2 mins 20 secs (1000W), 3 mins (800W), or until the butter melts and the milk is hot.

Mash until smooth and fluffy and adjust the seasoning to taste.

Micro-tips —— For extra creamy mash, you can use an electric whisk to beat the potatoes.

Topping Mix

Makes 4 tbsp
Ready in under 5 mins

2 tbsp ground paprika
3 tsp dried parsley
1½ tsp ground turmeric
1 tsp flaked sea salt or ½ tsp fine salt
1 tsp coarsely ground black pepper

Use this quick topping to add colour to any cheesy pasta or creamy potato dishes – basically anything that you might have baked or popped under the grill, in other circumstances. It will really help to give an appetising colour to the recipe and can be kept in a small jar to sprinkle over things whenever you like.

Put all the ingredients in a small jar, screw on the lid and shake well.

Use roughly ¼ tsp of the mixture to sprinkle over a family-sized dish.

Crunchy Topping Mix

Makes 10 tbsp
Ready in under 5 mins

50g ready-made croutons,
    from a packet
3 tsp dried parsley
½ tsp ground paprika
¼ tsp ground turmeric

Sprinkle this special mix over any savoury dishes that you would normally bake, such as macaroni cheese, to add a golden crunchy topping.

Put the croutons in a food processor or pestle and mortar and blitz or pound until crushed without becoming too powdery.

Add the herbs and spices and mix well.

Transfer to a jar, seal tightly and set aside until needed.

Pink Pickled Onion

Serves 4
Ready in 10 mins, plus cooling

1 medium red onion, peeled and
    very finely sliced into rings
3 tsp caster sugar
3 tsp red wine vinegar

A fantastic topping for pulled pork, burgers or chilli. Keep covered in the fridge and use within 3 days.

Put the onion in a medium microwaveable bowl and add 1 tbsp cold water. Cover and cook on HIGH for 4 mins (1000W), 5 mins (800W), or until the onion is softened, stirring halfway.

Stir in the sugar and vinegar – the onion should become a lot pinker when the vinegar is added. Season with a pinch of salt and a little ground black pepper. Leave to cool for around 30 mins before serving.

)))

Micro-tips —— If you don't have any red wine vinegar, use white wine vinegar or cider vinegar instead.

Apple Sauce

Serves 4
Ready in under 10 mins

2 medium cooking apples (around
    400g total weight), peeled,
    cored and cut into roughly
    2–3cm chunks
50g caster sugar
15g butter, cubed
generous pinch of salt

Home-made apple sauce is so much better than the shop-bought kind and is a cinch to make in the microwave. If you have a glut of cooking apples, make several batches as they will keep well in the freezer for up to six months.

Mix all the ingredients in a medium microwaveable bowl. Cover and cook on HIGH for 4 mins (1000W), 5 mins (800W), or until the apples are very soft, stirring halfway.

Mash lightly with a fork and leave to cool before serving.

Home-made Lemon Curd

Makes 200ml
Ready in under 10 mins

40g unsalted butter, cubed
60g caster sugar
1 large whole egg
1 large egg yolk
juice of 2–3 lemons (around 70ml juice)

A perfectly smooth lemon curd with just the right amount of zing. Spread thickly onto freshly buttered bread or use as a delicious filling for cakes and biscuits. This recipe makes a small jar – perfect for eating up in a few days – but feel free to double if you have a few lemons to use up.

Put the butter into a medium microwaveable bowl and cook on HIGH for 20 secs (1000W) or 30 secs (800W), until melted.

Add the sugar, whole egg and egg yolk and whisk until thoroughly combined. Stir in the lemon juice.

Cover and cook on HIGH for 1 min 30 secs (1000W) or 2 mins (800W), whisking every 30 secs, until the lemon curd is thickened to the consistency of custard and leaves a light trail when the spoon is lifted. It will continue to thicken as it cools.

Immediately pour the hot lemon curd into a warmed, very clean jar or bowl and leave to cool. Cover the curd with a disc of non-stick baking paper, to prevent a skin forming. Seal with a lid or cover the bowl. Keep in the fridge and use within 4–5 days.

Micro-tip —— It's very
important not to overheat the curd or the eggs could scramble. If you think it's still a little runny after cooking, continue in 20 sec increments. If doubling up the ingredients, increase the cooking time.

Proper Vanilla Custard

Serves 6
Ready in under 10 mins

10g (2 heaped tsp) cornflour

250ml whole milk

2 large egg yolks

25g caster sugar

1 vanilla pod, split lengthways and
the seeds scraped out with the
tip of a knife

250ml double cream

Making a proper custard in the microwave is easy and it takes away all the worry of overcooking the eggs. If you don't have any vanilla pods, use 1 tsp vanilla bean paste or good-quality vanilla extract.

Mix the cornflour with 1 tbsp of the milk in a medium microwaveable bowl. Add the egg yolks, sugar and vanilla seeds, extract or paste. Mix together thoroughly with a wooden spoon.

Pour in the remaining milk and the cream and mix well. Cook uncovered on HIGH for 4 mins (1000W) or 5 mins (800W), stirring after 3 mins, then stirring after every 30 secs until smooth and thickened. The custard will continue to thicken as it stands and cools, so don't be tempted to overcook it.

Serve straight away, or cover the surface of the custard with non-stick baking paper or film to prevent a skin forming. Any leftover custard can be kept covered in the fridge for up to 2 days. Reheat very gently, stirring regularly, to serve.

Micro-tip —— If you
think the eggs are on the verge of overcooking (you'll see a hint of graininess appear), transfer immediately to a cold bowl to halt the cooking process.

Hot Chocolate Sauce

Serves 4–6
Ready in under 5 mins

100ml double cream
100g plain (around 55% cocoa
    solids), milk or white chocolate,
    roughly chopped

This chocolate sauce can be made using dark, white or milk chocolate and is perfect for pouring over ice cream or any other dessert that calls for a wickedly rich sauce. Try with a banana split, profiteroles, microwave pancakes or waffles.

Put the cream and 2 tbsp water in a medium microwaveable bowl and mix. Cook uncovered on HIGH for 1 min (1000W) or 1 min 10 secs (800W), until hot but not boiling.

Stir in the chopped chocolate and mix until the sauce is smooth and glossy. The heat of the cream should melt the chocolate as you stir. (You can return the bowl to the microwave for a few seconds, if it needs to melt a little more.)

Serve warm.

Micro-tip —— Keep any leftovers covered in the fridge for up to a week. The sauce will thicken as it cools but can be easily reheated in the microwave for a few seconds.

Salted Caramel Sauce

Serves 4
Ready in under 5 mins

100ml double cream
50g soft light brown sugar
25g butter, cubed
generous pinch of flaked sea salt

A very simple sauce that's fantastic poured over ice cream or drizzled over microwave pancakes or waffles. The sea salt cuts through the sweetness of the sauce perfectly but if you don't have any handy, you can leave it out altogether or add a squeeze of lemon juice instead.

Put the cream, sugar and butter into a microwaveable bowl or jug – it will need to hold at least 300ml liquid, as the sauce will rise in the dish as it simmers.

Cook on HIGH for 1 min (1000W), 1 min 10 secs (800W), or until the butter melts and the sugar dissolves.

Leave to stand for 3 mins.

Stir in the flaked sea salt and serve.

COOKING KIT & TECHNIQUES

COOKING KIT

The great thing about microwave cooking is that you probably already have a lot of dishes that you need. And, if not, it's usually easy to pick up microwaveable containers in the supermarket, department stores, hardware shops, or online. Even charity shops often have Pyrex-style dishes, made from toughened glass, that can be used in the microwave. Here are a few of my favourite dishes and other essential additions to your kitchen cupboards and drawers:

TOUGHENED GLASS BOWLS

These mixing bowls are made from a particular type of glass called borosilicate. It's what Pyrex bowls are made from, but there are plenty of other manufacturers of this kind of bowl, too. These can be heated to high temperatures, can go in the freezer and dishwasher – and are brilliant for microwave cooking. I particularly like them for preparing cakes, as it means you can quickly soften butter in the microwave and then mix the cake in the same container. Large ones are best, so you have room to add other ingredients, but a couple of medium bowls are useful, too (for melting chocolate, for instance).

If you think you are going to use your microwave oven for cooking pasta, you'll need to buy an extra large bowl, that will hold around 3 litres, so the water won't boil over. I've also recommended a particular sized bowl, if you want to poach eggs. After cooking more than 30 eggs, this is what worked best for me, but with a bit of tweaking you may find that you already have the ideal dish.

Look out for bowls with lids, as it's a great way to avoid using film to cover dishes, but don't seal tightly when you cover as the steam generated by cooking will need to escape.

TOUGHENED GLASS CASSEROLES

These containers are game changers! Readily available and incredibly versatile, you can use them for anything from Bolognese to shepherd's pie, risottos and even cakes. Not only can you see what's happening in the dish as it cooks, you can also bring it straight to the table. The most useful casserole will hold at least 2.5 litres, but smaller ones are handy for single servings. And the lids can be upturned and used as plates for microwaving fish, chicken breasts or burgers, where juices can collect.

PIE AND OVEN DISHES

This is the kind of dish that you are likely to have already. If it's not already marked for microwave use, you can test whether it is suitable following the instructions on page 11. Round dishes are most useful, as they tend to work better with turntables.

If you don't have a turntable in your microwave, you have a bit more flexibility when it comes to shape – rectangle dishes can work well but you'll need to turn the dish at least once during cooking to avoid cold spots. Pie dishes shouldn't be too deep – as with all microwave cooking, shallow dishes work best, so ingredients can be spread out over the base. Avoid dishes that are narrow and deep. Pie dishes are unlikely to come with a lid, so you will need to cover with a plate or plastic film to prevent splatters (microwave-safe and ideally compostable film). Pie dishes aren't suitable for recipes that contain a lot of liquid as the sides aren't high enough and the liquid can boil over during cooking.

I often set my pie dishes on a microwaveable dinner plate, in case of any drips, and because it makes it easier to lift the dish in and out of the oven. Don't forget that hot food will heat the dishes too.

RAMEKINS

A set of four ramekins is a handy addition if you are a keen baker – or want to cook cakes more easily. I find that those holding around 175ml are the most useful.

You can use them just as they are for small desserts, or line with cupcake or muffin cases for cooking individual sponge cakes and muffins. The ceramic sides will hold the mixture in place so the cakes cook evenly – they can also sit straight onto a set of scales if you like to weigh your cake batter before cooking for really reliable results.

Cooking cupcakes and muffins in the microwave rather than a batch of twelve in the oven saves on energy costs as well as time. And it's a great way to introduce children to baking (with guidance from an adult).

MEASURING JUG

A 600ml microwaveable measuring jug is useful for melting, but a 1.2 litre jug is more handy, as you can use it for making all sorts of sauces without worrying about the liquid boiling over. From experience, I know that measurements on the side of jugs can be hard to read accurately, so I always put my jug on the scales to weigh liquids. It makes a lot of sense when you realise

that 1g is the same as 1ml for watery liquids, such as stock or wine. (It isn't the same for yoghurt or anything thick.)

I prefer the toughened glass jugs as they are sturdier, but microwaveable plastic jugs also work.

SILICONE BAKEWARE

Silicone bakeware is brilliant for microwave cooking and a worthwhile investment if you are tempted by the 'bakes' in this book. I tend to oil generously or line with non-stick baking paper, not because the cake mixtures get baked on, but because they are so light and fluffy, they can sometimes stick to the sides.

The most useful shape is a loaf 'tin' – sometimes labelled 22cm and holding about the same as a 900g traditional loaf tin. I also have 20cm and 23cm round silicone 'tin' moulds for cakes. The loaf is the most useful because its relatively narrow width means cakes cook extremely effectively.

MINI PUDDING BASINS

If you are a fan of little steamed sponge puddings, it's worth purchasing a set of individual pudding basins. You won't be able to use the metal kind in your microwave but plastic or toughened glass work well. The cooking times may vary slightly between them, though, so stick to one set and be prepared to adjust the recipe a little.

Weigh the batter into the basins to ensure each one contains the same amount and arrange them spaced evenly apart in the microwave for the most reliable results.

DISHES WITH VENTED LIDS

Look out for a new breed of microwaveable bowls and dishes with vented lids. These, again, are often made of toughened glass but can be plastic, too. Aimed often at people taking home-prepared meals to work for reheating, the larger ones are great for cooking and reheating, and the vented tabs can be closed up to keep food airtight in the fridge or freezer.

MICROWAVE COVER

Plastic covers specifically for the microwave are handy for covering food on plates or other shallow dishes and stop you having to rely on plastic film. If you don't have one, you could use a large upturned microwaveable mixing bowl; but you'll need to take care as they can get hot from the steam generated through the cooking process. Always use a dry cloth to protect your hands when you lift the cover off the food.

KITCHEN PAPER

Paper towel is useful for absorbing steam or liquid from food as it cooks – microwave cooking is a moist method and can create a large amount of steam that remains in the oven cavity.

Make sure you only use plain, microwave-safe kitchen paper that is NOT recycled, as some recycled paper can contain tiny fragments of metal or other materials that may begin sparking in the microwave. Check the packaging to see whether it can be used in the microwave and, if in doubt, leave it out.

Only use kitchen towel in a single layer when cooking foods that release lots of steam so it doesn't dry out. (Dry kitchen paper could ignite – check your microwave manufacturer's guidelines.)

Paper towel is also useful for wiping around the oven cavity and door after cooking to remove the condensation. Surprisingly, it's often foods that you wouldn't expect to create a lot of steam, such as cakes, that call for a quick wipe before you shut the door.

For extra information on how to clean your microwave oven, see my tips at www.justinepattison.com or refer to your manufacturer's handbook.

PLASTIC FILM & BAGS

I try very hard not to use any kind of plastic film in the microwave, as it is hard to recycle, but I have discovered a compostable one recently and there are likely to be more on the market over the next few years. If you use containers with lids or a microwave cover for your food, you shouldn't need to use any film at all, but it's handy for unusually shaped dishes and will help prevent liquids bubbling over the sides to some extent. I have also found microwave-safe roasting bags very handy for cooking my 'roast' chicken, and anything else that's an unusual shape. You can often pick them up in the supermarket.

NON-STICK BAKING PAPER

Although food doesn't get 'baked' onto surfaces in the same way as it does when something is oven cooked, non-stick baking paper is handy for cooking high-sugar recipes, such as biscuits, as food can be lifted off it more easily. I also use it for lining silicone bakeware, as it's useful for removing delicate sponges and other cakes from the moulds. Cakes cooked in the microwave are often more delicate than those cooked in the oven because they don't form a firm crust in the same way. I prefer to use the pre-cut liners but you can easily cut your own to fit.

COCKTAIL STICKS & SKEWERS

I always keep some cocktail sticks handy for pricking chicken or fish fillets that could 'pop' in the microwave. I tend to prick the thinner ends or sides of chicken breasts, as it helps avoid the pressure build up caused by steam. It's not an infallible technique, though, so if your chicken or fish does begin to 'pop', simply stop the microwave for a short while to allow the heat to redistribute and then continue.

Skewers are handy for testing the doneness of some cakes – and you can also use the tip for pricking potatoes, or for chicken and fish if you don't have cocktail sticks.

Testing for doneness with a skewer doesn't work for everything, though, as depending on the mixture and shape of your cooking container, you could find that the wettest parts are on the outside rather than in the centre. If you are unsure and your cake has had the correct cooking time, then insert the skewer into a couple of places. If it comes out clean, or with just a few crumbs clinging to the sides, the cake is likely to be ready.

DIGITAL KITCHEN SCALES

Electronic kitchen scales are a must-have in every kitchen for fool-proof results. Until you really become accustomed to microwave cooking, it's best to follow my recipes as accurately as possible, as the timings have been worked out very carefully. A set of kitchen scales will ensure you are on track and they are a cost-effective investment. And, if you have a sturdy set, you can pop your bowl on top and use it for both measuring and mixing, saving you time and washing up.

DIGITAL THERMOMETER

I am a huge fan of hand-held digital food thermometers and they are particularly useful for microwave cookery, as the timings are short, there could be cold spots, and you can't rely on appearance to judge whether a dish is finished in quite the same way as you can with traditional oven- or hob-cooked food. Simply probe deeply in several places with the end of the thermometer into any food that needs to be hot throughout (I'm thinking particularly of chicken and reheated food). So long as it is reading 75°C or above, your dish should be safe to eat. If not, return to the microwave and continue cooking.

Microwave ovens vary, too, so although the recipes in this book have been tested in a variety of ovens, having a digital thermometer to hand means you can quickly and easily check cooking times for your particular model – just jot any tweaks on the recipe page for next time.

MEASURING SPOONS

All the recipes in this book have been tested using sets of measuring spoons for the most accurate results. Spoons from a cutlery drawer can vary enormously, so a set of proper measuring spoons will help ensure success. You can pick them up very easily in the cookware section of the supermarket, department stores, cookware shops and online. Unless otherwise stated, measuring spoon amounts are always level.

TECHNIQUES

Microwave cookery does call for a few specific techniques – and in order to keep the recipes as concise as possible, I've gathered a collection of handy tips and tricks here.

BEEF, LAMB & PORK

As meat cooks very quickly in the microwave, fat doesn't really have time to soften and large chunks can easily toughen. Also the meat won't brown as there is no contact with a hot surface.

Ultimately, all meat-based recipes have been created with a certain degree of compromise but they are all, nevertheless, quick, convenient and very delicious!

For the best results, choose lean cuts to start with and trim off any excess fat, as much as possible. Beef and pork are generally fairly easy to trim but lamb can be more problematic.

To help keep the meat tender, slice it thinly widthways, working your way up a steak, rather than lengthways, cutting across the grain, in order to keep the meat fibres short. Cutting into strips like this means the meat remains tender to eat and a little goes a long way.

All the recipes call for a full power setting (also referred to as 100%, depending on your oven) and cooking for longer won't tenderise meat any further, so follow the recipes and keep the timings short, even if you can't initially see the rationale.

It is possible to cook meat casseroles longer at a lower power, but unless there is a particular reason to do so, it's probably not worth it. But do check your microwave manufacturer's handbook.

MINCE

Mince, whatever the kind, works very well in the microwave, but it's worth sticking to the techniques I've recommended, whether staged cooking or seasoning tips.

Whenever you cook mince in the microwave, it's really important to break up the meat between bouts of cooking. This is because the mince will cook quickly into a lump if it isn't separated at least once during the cooking process.

To get the best results, I use two wooden spatulas or spoons and crush the mince as much as I can using a vertical chopping action (see photo on page 15). You would do this anyway if you were browning the mince in a pan on the hob, but this way it's done in just one or two stages.

CHICKEN & TURKEY

Cuts of chicken, whether breasts or thighs, should always be skinless, unless you are starting the meat off in a frying pan and only finishing with microwave power.

For the recipes in this book, you will need to trim off any fat or sinew. I always do this carefully with a good set of kitchen scissors. Either cut the chicken into small, evenly sized chunks, or cut into long strips for quick cooking and tender results. Keep pieces spaced apart, if possible, while they cook, and stir or turn regularly.

Whole breasts can be flattened to ensure even cooking or thinner ends pierced several times with a cocktail stick to help prevent 'popping' as the chicken cooks. Only cook one or two breasts at a time for the best results. And only use smaller whole birds to help ensure even cooking.

FISH & SEAFOOD

Fish and seafood cooks wonderfully quickly using microwave power, so the most important thing is not to overcook it. You will probably find that any recipe you normally follow to steam or bake fish will work in the microwave, but anything that has a crust or a batter will end up soggy, due to the moist heat generated. Fish fillets do have a tendency to 'pop' a little sometimes, so don't forget to prick any thinner ends, or fold them under the thicker parts of the fillets. And cook in two stages if you can, stopping roughly halfway through the cooking time for a short while to allow the heat to redistribute. If cooking prawns, scallops or other small seafood, make sure you stir regularly to ensure even cooking, especially if you have a microwave oven without a turntable.

VEGETABLES

The most important thing to remember for vegetables is to keep the size consistent for the most reliable results. Cooking times will be quicker for smaller vegetable pieces than larger, and vegetables spread over a wide base will cook more quickly and efficiently than those piled into a smaller dish several pieces deep.

Vegetables with a high water content, such as tomatoes or courgettes, will cook more rapidly than root vegetables, such as swede or beetroot.

Don't forget to stir vegetables as they cook, in case there are any cold spots in your oven. And

it's important to remember that you won't need anywhere near as much water as you would use on the hob. Usually just a splash is enough for green vegetables and not much more for dense vegetables, such as carrots, potatoes or parsnips.

For lots of vegetable recipes and ideas, visit my website **www.justinepattison.com**

PASTA & RICE

In many cases, it makes more sense to cook pasta or rice on the hob. But if you only want one or two portions, cooking in the microwave can be helpful, especially if you want to add an easy sauce to pasta or want to leave a rice dish cooking while you get on with something else. Pasta and rice will take a similar amount of time to cook in whatever wattage of microwave you use. In every recipe I use either just-boiled water from the kettle or hot stock, to reduce the amount of time it takes for the microwave energy to heat a large volume of water.

The key to cooking pasta or rice successfully in a microwave is to ensure you use a large enough bowl or casserole. The starchy water will boil up and if your container isn't large enough, it will bubble over the sides. It's also important to stir at least once during the cooking process. I've tried out a couple of microwave rice cookers without much success, so feel that a decent-sized bowl and a lid is the best way to go.

Italian cooks will probably be horrified to learn that I've found that adding a couple of teaspoons of oil to the water will help subdue the most vigorous bubbling and prevent boil-over in many cases.

Cooking pasta is the one time that I'm most likely to use microwave-safe plastic film to cover my bowl. I find that it expands with the steam from the boiling water and helps prevent liquid from running down the sides of the bowl or dish. I always place my bowl on a microwaveable plate to catch any wayward drips, too.

Be aware that any dish used to cook pasta or rice will be extremely hot, so be careful to prevent spills and remove lids so the steam rises away from you. This all might sound a bit scary, but following this simple guidance will help you make fantastic dishes with very little bother.

FRUIT

All fruit will cook quickly using microwave power as it has such a high water content. As with vegetables, scatter the fruit over a wide-based dish, rather than heaping it into a smaller bowl. And only add a couple of tablespoons of water. Cover before cooking and check regularly – berries in particular will soften very quickly. Add sugar to taste, if needed, at the end of the cooking time.

SWEET BAKES

Baking in the truest sense isn't possible unless you own a combination microwave, but the cakes in this book work brilliantly and friends and family will be amazed.

You'll notice that sponges don't have the golden colour that you might usually associate with a cake as there is no browning. But they do cook incredibly quickly – under 5 minutes in most cases – and remain light and moist. It is still possible to overcook them, though, so follow my timings and be ready to tweak by a few seconds to suit your microwave.

If they do overcook, you'll find the cake or biscuits tend to harden before overbrowning so you may not notice initially, as the colour is unlikely to show on the surface of the cake itself. So watch carefully

the first time you bake and be prepared to adjust if necessary.

To check it's ready, look at the edges of the cake, which should be a little damp without being raw, as the mixture will continue cooking for a short while after the microwave stops. Press the surface of the cake gently and it should feel fairly firm and spring back.

Biscuits and cookies will continue to crisp up as they cool, so don't be tempted to cook for longer – sometimes the very inside of the biscuit will start overbrowning while the outside remains pale. I always break one biscuit in half when cooking in an unfamiliar microwave to see what is going on inside before 'baking' the rest of the batch, and adjust my timings accordingly.

SAVOURY BAKES

When cooking savoury bakes, such as macaroni cheese or lasagne, you will notice that the top doesn't brown with microwave power alone. To make the dishes in this book look more traditional, I've created a couple of toppings that you can keep in a screw top jar and dip into whenever you need (see page 211).

You'll also find that ready-made croutons and crostini add colour and crunch to bakes and help mimic the appearance and taste of oven-baked dishes. And, of course, you can always pop a microwave 'bake' under a hot grill at the end of the cooking time if you wish.

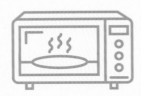

HOW MICROWAVES COOK FOOD

Now for the science... Did you know that the microwave energy the ovens are named after is actually found in the atmosphere all the time, both naturally and via man-made sources, such as radios, televisions and mobile phones?

- In a microwave oven, electricity is converted into microwave energy by a magnetron.

- This energy bounces off the metal walls of the oven and the metal mesh door screen.

- It passes through cooking containers, as light passes through a window, and is absorbed by water molecules in the food. It is able to penetrate food to a depth of around 4–5cm.

- The microwaves cause the water molecules to vibrate, which produces heat, and this cooks the food.

MICROWAVE COOKING CHART

I've created this guide to help you work out cooking times for my recipes if you have a 700W or 900W microwave oven. There should be a label on the front or just inside the door of your oven. If yours has a wattage that isn't listed below, simply choose the one closest to it.

I've rounded the calculations up or down a few seconds in some cases, so they are easier to follow. You may find that your microwave is trickier to program (if it has a dial rather than buttons), or the increments might be different. As long as you use the timings as a guide, you will be able to follow the recipes, just remember you may need to tweak them a little. I suggest you jot down any changes you needed to make for your oven alongside a recipe, so you don't have to work out the timings another time.

On the whole, I recommend rounding down rather than up when adapting the figures, because you can always add extra time but rescuing something that has been over cooked is a whole lot more difficult.

As always, don't forget to turn the dish regularly if your microwave oven doesn't have a turntable, to help ensure even cooking and bear in mind that foods will continue cooking for a short while once the microwave energy stops.

For additional advice, refer to the manufacturer's instruction booklet.

700W		800W		900W		1000W	
mins	sec	mins	sec	mins	sec	mins	sec
	10		10		10		10
	25		20		15		15
	35		30		25		25
	45		40		35		30
	55		50		45		40
1	10	1	0		50		50
1	40	1	30	1	15	1	10
2	15	2	0	1	40	1	35
2	50	2	30	2	10	2	0
3	25	3	0	2	35	2	25
3	55	3	30	3	0	2	50
4	30	4	0	3	25	3	10
5	5	4	30	3	50	3	35
5	40	5	0	4	15	4	0
6	10	5	30	4	40	4	25
6	45	6	0	5	10	4	50
7	20	6	30	5	35	5	10
7	55	7	0	6	0	5	35
8	25	7	30	6	25	6	0
9	0	8	0	6	50	6	25
9	35	8	30	7	15	6	50
10	10	9	0	7	40	7	10
10	50	9	30	8	5	7	35
11	15	10	0	8	30	8	0

CONVERSION CHARTS

WEIGHT

Metric	Imperial	Metric	Imperial
10g	¼oz	375g	13oz
15g	½oz	400g	14oz
20g	¾oz	425g	15oz
25g	1oz	450g	16oz (1lb)
40g	1½oz	500g (0.5kg)	1lb 2oz
50g	2oz	550g	1¼lb
60g	2¼oz	600g	1lb 5oz
70g	2¾oz	675g	1½lb
75g	3oz	725g	1lb 10oz
100g	3½oz	800g	1¾lb
115g	4oz	850g	1lb 14oz
125g	4½oz	900g	2lb
140g	4¾oz	1kg	2¼lb
150g	5oz	1.1kg	2½lb
160g	5½oz	1.25kg	2¾lb
175g	6oz	1.3kg	3lb
200g	7oz	1.5kg	3¼lb
225g	8oz	1.6kg	3½lb
250g	9oz	1.8kg	4lb
275g	9½oz	2kg	4½lb
300g	11oz	2.25kg	5lb
350g	12oz	2.5kg	5½lb

VOLUME

Metric	Imperial	Metric	Imperial
125ml	¼ tsp	375ml	13 fl oz
2.5ml	½ tsp	400ml	14 fl oz
5ml	1 tsp	450ml	15 fl oz (¾ pint)
15ml	1 tbsp	475ml	16 fl oz (1 US pint)
30ml	1 fl oz (2 tbsp)	500ml	18 fl oz
50ml	2 fl oz	600ml	20 fl oz (1 UK pint)
75ml	3 fl oz	700ml	1¼ pints (25 fl oz)
100ml	2 fl oz	850ml	1½ pints (30 fl oz)
125ml	4 fl oz	1 litre	1¾ pints (35 fl oz)
150ml	5 fl oz (¼ UK pint)	1.2 litres	2 pints (40 fl oz)
175ml	6 fl oz	1.3 litres	2¼ pints
200ml	7 fl oz	1.4 litres	2½ pints
250ml	8 fl oz	1.75 litres	3 pints
275ml	9 fl oz	2 litres	3½ pints
300ml	10 fl oz (½ imperial pint)	3 litres	5 pints
325ml	11 fl oz		
350ml	12 fl oz		

SPOONS (LIQUIDS)

Metric	Imperial
1 tsp	5 ml
2 dsp	10 ml
1 tbsp (3 tsp)	15 ml

INDEX

ACKNOWLEDGEMENTS

A HUGE THANK YOU

Huge thanks to everyone who enjoys my recipes and the way I cook. You have given me such fantastic feedback; I hope you like my microwave recipes just as much! Join my Justine Pattison Recipe Chat group on Facebook if you'd like to share ideas and photos of what you've cooked and get involved in my live Q&A sessions.

And now back to the brilliant people who have helped created this book. Firstly, the amazing Claire Bignell and Karen Brooks for their superb organisational and creative skills; for helping keep the project on track and for months of brainstorming, recipe testing and photo shoot assistance. I really don't know what I would have done without you both!

I'm truly grateful to the very talented photographer Kate Whitaker for not only the wonderful photographs but also selecting the perfect props and helping make the recipes look both beautiful and achievable.

For Jo Roberts-Miller, my Project Editor, for her constant encouragement and enthusiasm for Ping! For being a great sounding-board and helping me stick to all the deadlines. It meant so much that you were inspired enough to cook a few of the recipes for your family as you worked on them.

At HQ, I would like to start by thanking Lisa Milton and Louise McKeever who loved the idea of Ping! right from the beginning and were happy to follow my vision. I hope you are as happy with the book as I am. Thanks also to my fantastic editor Nira Begum for her guidance and for helping facilitate my ideas in such a kind and considered way.

Big thanks to Georgie Hewitt for designing the book so beautifully. You've helped bring microwave cooking bang up to date with your inspirational design – and I love the simplicity of the pages; making the book not only look great but also so inviting to read and cook from.

I'm also grateful to my agent, Rory Scarfe, for being excited by the potential of this project. And the rest of the team at The Blair Partnership, including Hattie Grünewald and Clara Foster, and the Legal and Rights Team at TBP for looking after the business side of things so efficiently.

And a special shout-out for all my 'Micro-Wavers'. Your feedback on the recipes has been invaluable – and I can't thank you enough!

And, of course, an enormous thank you to my family, John, Jess and Emily, for your input and enthusiasm for my microwave recipes – however many times you tried them.

For Becca Spry

HQ
An imprint of HarperCollins*Publishers* Ltd
1 London Bridge Street
London SE1 9GF

www.harpercollins.co.uk

HarperCollins*Publishers*
Macken House,
39/40 Mayor Street Upper,
Dublin 1, D01 C9W8

10 9 8 7 6 5 4 3 2 1

First published in Great Britain by HQ, an imprint of
HarperCollins*Publishers* Ltd 2023

Text copyright © Justine Pattison 2023

Justine Pattison asserts the moral right to be identified
as the author of this work. A catalogue record for this book
is available from the British Library.

ISBN: 978-0-00-858016-2

For more information visit: www.harpercollins.co.uk/green
Photographer: Kate Whitaker
Food styling: Justine Pattison
Food assistants: Claire Bignell and Karen Brooks
Prop styling: Kate Whitaker
Project Editor: Jo Roberts-Miller
Senior Editor: Nira Begum
Book Design: Georgie Hewitt
Production: Halema Begum

Printed and bound in Italy by ROTOLITO S.p.A.

Microwave ovens vary and although great care has been
taken creating the recipes for this book, it is important that
you follow your microwave manufacturer's instructions for
the safest results. If you no longer have the manual, you may
be able to download it online or receive advice from the
manufacturer's website. The author and publishers accept no
responsibility for the use or misuse of any microwave oven.

The recipes are a guide to timings and may need to be
adjusted according to your microwave oven. Do not allow
foods to overheat.

Check that containers are suitable for use in a microwave
oven before use. Use the size and shape of bowls and
dishes recommended in the recipes for the best results.
Any variation will result in changes to the cooking times.
Be aware that compact microwave ovens may not be
suitable for cooking larger dishes.

Dishes cooked in the microwave can get very hot. Ensure
care is taken when moving hot dishes, especially when they
contain large quantities of liquid. Food and liquids should
not be heated in sealed containers.

All dairy ingredients, eggs and perishable foods used
in testing these recipes have been stored in the fridge
at 5C. If using from room temperature, or cooking soon
after purchase, you may need to reduce cooking times.

Always use a digital food thermometer after cooking
food, especially if it was made using raw meat or poultry,
to ensure it has reached a safe eating temperature.